Memoirs of a World War I Nurse

Memoirs of a World War I Nurse

Nora Elizabeth Daly
(Posthumously)

iUniverse, Inc.
Bloomington

Memoirs of a World War I Nurse

iUniverse books may be ordered through booksellers or by contacting:

iUniverse
1663 Liberty Drive
Bloomington, IN 47403
www.iuniverse.com
1-800-Authors (1-800-288-4677)

ISBN: 978-1-4620-4350-7 (sc)
ISBN: 978-1-4620-4351-4 (ebk)

Printed in the United States of America

iUniverse rev. date: 10/06/2011

Preface

    This was written by my beautiful mother, Nora Elizabeth Daly. It started out as her diary during World War I, where she was a nurse in France. But as you read on I feel you will find much more. All the places she went to and the things that happened are so elaborately told; such as her visits to Monte Carlo and the Notre Dame Cathedral in France, and so many other places and situations and her description of the friendly French people. To me it is not just a diary but an education on certain places in Europe and yes it also tells the beautiful love story of my mother and father, who met during their service—my mother as a nurse and my father a doctor. Their everyday experiences in war and in love are most eloquently described. Thank you mom for your love and your beautiful diary.

Monte Carlo

Monte Carlo closely populated in high season, sits on the radiant azure coast, shining at night like a crown of royal jewels tossed down by the sea-sophistication itself.

Yet up in mysterious mountains behind its rock villages are people with descendants of Saracen pirates; there are fortresses where the peasant's dogs "go wolf," old hidden towns with churches that cherish treasures of the crusades, and customs that haven't changed in centuries. If there hadn't been danger of the Franco Prussian War probably Monaco would still remain the poverty-stricken principality it was after its revolution of over fifty years ago, when Roquebrune and Newton were rift from its (then) tyrant ruler. All the gay gamblers would still have been running to Hamburg or Baden-Baden where a certain astute Monsieur Francoise Blanc, locally called Herr Weiss, offered brilliant attractions. In the sixties with war talk in the air and an inspiration for "cleaning things up" this gentleman was earnestly persuaded to leave Germany. He had to go somewhere. There were several countries that didn't encourage him. Then one of his inspirations, what about Monaco. Prince and people were poor. Climate as well as scenery good. One might do something there.

The Grimaldi family, which ruled Monaco was one of the oldest and proudest in the world. But the nasty little revolution had reduced the principality to the size of a torn rug. Charles III lived in a wonderful palace, full of history and rats, in the rock of

Monaco where Hercules once was king. There was already a tiny gambling place there. But of no importance and practically no people. Monsieur Blanc talked diplomatically toward a good deal and a contract was signed, immensely beneficial to both parties.

It wasn't until 1898, however that a stock company was formed paying the prince at an increased ratio each year. At one time it was said that in 1937 the payments would amount to five million.

There are a few places along the southern part of Europe almost as popular as Monte Carlo though the above may not prove true. The casino (such as it was) reared itself upon the Rock also and gamblers arrived from Nice in boats. When success piled upon success a new casino rose in Monaco's principal town. Monte Carlo lower than the Rock and higher then the flat stretch of land between the two known as the Condamine. Monaco is divided into three parts, each very different from the other. On the Rock is the prince's palace, ancient with middle age tradition, the palace of the Governor, the court of Justice, the Byzantine Cathedral, the famous fish museum of the scientific loving Prince Albert, and I think the largest and finest aquarium in the world. Both the cathedral and the museum were built with money received from that contract with the Blanc family, which is now related by marriage to half the royalty of Europe.

A few fine big villas belonging to rich Monegasques and hundreds of old huddled homes leaning against each other in narrow tumbled streets. On the Rock live the ancient aristocracy—or what's left of it. It's a good thing for sojourners at Monte Carlo that there weren't more because the ancient aristocracy who got most of the tickets for the gorgeous operas, ballets, plays and classical events at the casino theaters. They and the wives of the croupier's, many of whom also abide on that exclusive Rock where few if any foreigners are allowed to dwell.

Above is a photo of the Prince's palace on "The Rock."

The "Societe des Baines de Mer" S.B.M. as the controllers of the Casino, sweetly call themselves, spend untold thousands in bringing to Monte Carlo the best singers, dancers, actors and musicians of the world. A wonderful advertisement for Monte Carlo to have these splendid attractions. Its another inducement to visit Monte Carlo—like the glorious golf course far above, La Turbie (500 meters above sea level), perhaps the most spectacular golf course on earth. So much for the Rock its dark eyed dandily dressed jeweled aristocracy-it's Saracenic-Italian patios and it's canny croupiers—who mostly own shops and apartment houses in the Condamine or even if they are of a saving disposition, shops and small hotels it glittering Monte Carlo itself.

People use to say these croupiers were "mostly Germans" before the war. They never were. They were always far more Mongasques, Frenchmen and Italians with a sprinkling of nearly all white races except the English and Americans. Down underground, where nobody sees or knows of it, is the croupiers school. They have to attend six months before they can become real croupiers spinning roulette wheels, or dealing (trente-et-quarante) cards.

They are calm, nerve—proof men coming on duty at 10:00 a.m. in coats without pockets, impolitely supplied by the S.B.M going home at midnight after a long day, two hours on—two hours off. In the underground school, young candidates not only learn how to spin, deal and so forth but to withstand any sudden shock. You see though its considered most caddish to kill yourself inside the casino, and in fact, none of the best suicides ever do it, a very few bounders have thus forgotten their manners and it takes some nerve to go on as if nothing had happened, with a slight spatter of some one else's brains on your shirt front, through the night someone else has been whisked away-even in the famous earthquake season of over 30 years ago, a croupier must not lose his nerve. Neither hand or voice must tremble as play goes quietly on. They must have it in order to make good.

They're well paid, well treated, and well pensioned. Their families pensioned if they die and there was much of this in the war when every young man French, Italian, and Monegasque croupier went. The Casino would gladly have shut its doors to the public "for the duration" if all the trade people and hotel keepers of the Riviera had not implored the president. He said the Casino never sends a dime but it never forgets, and if after helping someone to get home, and he returns some years later, he is reminded of the little matter of $1,000 or so with interest.

Along the Corniche or Sea road there are scores of pretty villas tenanted by people whose names are always in the American newspapers. They're villas are paid for by the Casino and when they entertain visitors from the States who are principally know for the money they can spend, the Casino pays the bills.

Above is a picture of Prince Albert.

Thru Prince Albert, much of the Casino gold fund found its way into scientific research along the bottoms of the seven seas. The present Prince Louis II is content to receive his share of the Casino profits, a stipulated sum each year. To his credit he would close the Casino, if he dared. But Monte Carlo would wither and die without it's gambling palace.

Its buildings and landscape gardening are as beautiful as money can make them. It's trade is fine and the overly rich are welcomed and everything that can be done, to entertain them is done on a magnificent scale. Of course the Casino itself is finer then a king's adobe and the elegance of the theater approaches that of the opera house at Paris. The prince protects them from the rabble and in turn they fight for the privilege of leaving their gold in the green felt of his gaming tables. There are no taxes assessed against the inhabitants of his realm, which includes the city of Monte Carlo, because the gaming tables pay enough tribute to the city to meet all its expenses.

The prince knows that gambling at its best even where it is conducted without fraud, is a skin game, and in the end if persisted will ruin those who follow the will o' the wisp illusions. So the rule is that no inhabitant of his principality and no citizen of even so far away a places as Nice shall play at the tables of Monte Carlo. He does not want his people or those living nearby impoverished and so they are told to stay away from the tables. During the war and for sometime after the Armistice no one in uniform was allowed to play and the trips then were made early before the gambling started.

Ordinarily before entering one must have credentials sufficient to identify him as a non-resident. On entering the atrium which is a long hall connected with all the rooms and around it are twenty-eight Iconic marble columns on which is a gallery with railings, ornamented with vases and bronze chandeliers. There are several large gambling rooms connecting each other. They are adorned with fine paintings and in what is known as the Schmit room are sixteen pillars, eight of which are remarkable columns of agate, circled with bronze supporting a magnificent ceiling with arches decorated with sculptures. There are six large double roulette tables and one "trente et quante" table, measuring (30-40) which is a card game where minimum stakes is twenty francs, with a maximum stake of twelve thousand francs. Roulette is the favorite game. At these tables no person is permitted to stake less than five francs and no more than six thousand francs at each turn of the wheel. Money changers are located at handy points where chips might be cashed in. More women then men play. There is a large force of detectives in room always. Hotel men are frequently interviewed at Nice regarding people who sought diversions at Monte Carlo.

Jewels worn are safe in Casino. Quite often, however, jewels find their way from white throats to greasy fingers of the Messieurs les Preceurs, the pawn brokers whose shops are thick along the byways of the Casino square.

The superstitious gambler must have a mascotte and of course a pretty one. There are certain fixed rules. For example, it is forbidden for the employer to be sentimental with his mascotte. She must not be complimented upon her personal appearance, nor her gown. Their gowns by the way are usually furnished by Paris and London dressmakers as an advertisement, are as daring as they may be. The employer must not indulge in even a mild flirtation. This would hinder the mascotte's magic. The fee of the mascotte, who may be engaged for a single session of play or for a season, is fifteen percent of the winnings. She must be content in the very assurance of her own magic with no fee at all when her mystic influence upon the Gods of chance fail her and her employer quite the table of a loser. So in her way the way the mascotte is a gambler, too, though she does not risk a penny. If her employer loses in the end, she need only to remind him that he cast too admiring a glance at her on the way across the gardens to the Casino, and thus upset her magic. But what these charming, winsome girls can not do, is insure their own lives in a single year, not long ago, nine of them were cruelly murdered. Only four of the slayers were caught. These four were too stupid or crazed by their losses, to run away. And the police know of no approved method by which they may avoid arresting a murderer who refuses to run away. Each of the four slayers caught, accused his mascotte of having persuaded him against his will to remain at the tables, fighting against the bank, with hope that luck would turn. This is denied, for the mascotte who would deliberately break the rules against sentimental fascination or urge ruinous playing would be ostracized.

Still the loser at roulette continue to murder them and as a rule safely run away. The frail bodies that have earned such a cruel fee are tenderly laid away by their loyal friends, the priests of the little church of St. Devote. Devote is the Christian girl who was tortured by Kaiser, and buried in the valley, "Valley of Goumates," Monte Carlo's patron saint.

During the war Monte Carlo might have perished as a gamblers haven if Sir. Basil Zaharaoff former street urchin had not come to the rescue of Maurice Blanc. After the war, Zaharoff bought the Blanc interests and now owns the Casino and everything it supports. Behind everything that is Monte Carlo stands this silent inscrutable figure of the man of mystery, a street waif of Constantinople, who became a British baronet, husband of a Spanish duchess, dictator to Greece, Czeko-Slovakian and Estonia and the hope of the Romanoff's restoration to the throne of the Czars. In this romantic personality the gamblers gold of Monte Carlo links its human symbol. Intrigue, affecting the peace of nations, the comfort of society and the safety of homes mingle with the tragedy of money reflected in the faces and the surging crowds that move about the Hall of Games. Faces that represent every station of life, from English duchess to French cocotte, from cabinet ministers to Apache.

Over the ancient squares and crooked streets of Monte Carlo a ghostly army hovers, wraiths of a nation that was gambled away. In song and story Monaco was heroic until it became the place of evil setting the fashion of deceit and lust and avarice around the world.

Today it is said; the prince of Monaco rules a country into which the world's gold flows but he has lost his people. It is against the rules of the Casino for military or naval officers of any country to play at the gaming tables. Persons of official consequence may cause too much trouble if sufficiently disturbed by their losses. It is safer to do without their contributions. By the same reasoning no visitor known to be connected with a bank, a church, or a home for orphans, is granted admission to the Casino. One is not permitted to enter the Casino without a passport, particularly, a passport showing that the visitor is a New York slicker, it is recognized instantly by the Casino's management, as proof positive that the bearer is a wise old (bird) owl that is needed inside. Then he gets an admission ticket costing only a few cents.

A tourist's description of Monte Carlo: Most of the town and it's rock stands on end from the white surf of the cost line straight up to the jagged old peaks towering more than two-thousand feet almost directly above the municipal chimneys. Beginning down near the Casino a pile of ornate cream colored walls rambling low along the top of the first sea-edge terrace. Monte Carlo dashes itself bravely against the feet of the Maritime Alps in a long wave of yellowish buildings, all roofed with red tiles. Little villas gleaming high on the hills, the far-flung last drop of the waves' fruitless leap toward the summits. High over all a great tower of stone, built two-thousand years ago by Cesar, looks down from the clouds on the close clutter of wonderful shops, gay restaurants, long rambling hotels snuggling among the palms, olive and orange and lemon trees in mid-winter bloom eucalyptus and mimosa. The dazzling Hotel de Paris just outside the Casino, the café de Paris across the way and the International Sporting Club.

O.D. McIntyre gives another angle. The morning after the night before, as somehow seeming a tarnished toy. The streets filled with ghosts of last nights pleasure throngs. On the expansive sidewalks are mountainous piles of tables, chairs piled on one another, the debris of cigars and cigarette ends, broken cocktail glasses and burned out matches. Water carts and street cleaners, sweepers with their comic brooms are attacking the litter. Here and there are villainous looking rag pickers, unbelievably filthy and aged, making furtive selections along the terrace. Curtained and shuttered shops soon to be so vitally alive, present a blank gloom, and over it all is the sulking and brooding presence of the Casino. It is difficult to picture the desert waste as the place which was last night, strung with colored lights, throbbing with orchestras and filled with giddy fashionables from all parts of the world. A cathedral bell rings, but it seems to find no response.

From the terraces one can see faintly the snow clad peaks of the Corsican mountains. Below the terrace is the Tri-Crux-Pigons, Trap pigeon shooting is a daily event from ten to ten-thirty a.m. and attracts crack shots from all over the world. Near the post office is the thermal establishment, where every known sort of medicated bath may be taken. There is also a room where mineral waters from every health resort on the continent are on tap at normal temperature. This is so the cure commenced at any foreign spot may be continued. Monte Carlo seems to awaken at the same moment with everybody rushing out from hotels to amusements. Many make for sidewalk café tables and stiff jolts before breakfast are not unusual.

After the morning cleaning, Monte Carlo impresses you most for its scrupulous cleanliness and pin-like neatness. Monte Carlo's magnificent parade before lunch. It is a daily fashion show of what has been called the smartest dressed crowd in the world. Open carriages jog by with women occupants caring their tiny parasols. Men are in braided morning coats. Every texture of humanity from coarsest to finest, rub elbows. It is a hive of passion, disappointment, and strident joy. All its sordid ugliness is hidden with smothering grandeur. You can defend that at least one of the happy arrivals today will attempt a wretched suicide in a fortnight or so.

Later—Prince Pierre, the current ruler, may soon step down and award the governmental reins to his tiny, popular and beautiful daughter, Princess Antoinette. Princess "Tony" is a trifle young to be entrusted with cares of state—she is deeply beloved by the Monagasques. She may be able to heal lacerated feelings and reconcile warring parties, hitherto bitterly antagonistic. Prince Pierre's reign is threatened with disruption because it is believed he is entirely too much pro-Casino and does not exact adequate taxes from the Casino's interests. When she takes up the scepter, it is devoutly hoped that in addition to clipping the Casino's golden wings, the princess will issue orders against pigeon shooting. Reports of an impending revolution in Monaco tends to take on a musical—comedy aspect. The Monagasque standing army is twenty-four members strong.

*A picture of the sea cliffs of the promontory looking toward
the Grand Casino of Monte Carlo.*

Nice

Nice lies on the blue Mediterranean, picturesque and beautiful with the loveliest surroundings, the most beautiful city of Northern France. It has more then two hundred thousand inhabitants, has a five-mile promenade, beautiful bay and an ideal climate.

Old Nice is situated between the River Paillon and the sea. It is filled with narrow, torturous streets. The shops are dark and many are without windows. Merchandise is displayed in the street. All the upper stories of the buildings are flapping with wash. It is a place of excellent bargains, especially for antique collectors. At a roadside inn, sporting a tiny bar and four tables for two one may have sandwiches and beer for six totaling twenty-nine cents and a four cent tip for the inn-keeper leaving him delirious with joy. This is a peek at café life in France that is passing.

There are two especially beautiful drives over the mountains. The drive to Mentone, Monte Carlo, Eze and Monaco—known as the Coruishe drive is over a road that was first constructed by the Phoenicians. The Romans under Caesar reconstructed it and Napoleon I made it, in 1806, what it is today, the finest and smoothest of country highways—a most beautiful road with fine stone walls along the steep sides. Think the road was really started by Napoleon about 1796-98. The mountain tops, which stood as sentinels challenging the enemies of France, whether they might appear from the Mediterranean or at the Italian borders, bristled with military fortifications. There is a doubt whether bombs could materially disturb them, for they are tunneled into the granite of the mountains and are so spacious that these various forts can accommodate 100,000 soldiers. All the way up the slopes the wonderful vineyards, the fascinating houses clinging to the rocks, beauties and wonders at every turn—the air exquisite and the atmosphere as clear as crystal. This road extends from Naples, up, up Nice, far below and the lovely Mediterranean as blue as the sky.

The fine view of Monaco, where Prince Albert Louis rules over the smallest government in the world has no Parliament and its Army consists of 80 men. It may be smaller now. The highest point is at La Turbie, 500 meters above sea level, an old Roman town. Nearby are the remains of the tower Emperor Augustus built in 23 B.C. in celebration of the subjection of the Alpine tribes.

Grasse France

When Cannes, now the playground of the fashionable world of Europe and America was an unknown fishing village; Its next door neighbor on the Rivera, Grasse was a thriving city.

It is one of the oldest and most historic spots on the Mediterranean. In the Middle Ages it was a town of sufficient consequence to attract the unwelcome attention of the Saracens. For centuries it has been the scene of sackings and rebuilding by various kings and princes.

No one of the feminine gender comes to Cannes or Nice but gives a day for a visit to Grasse now a small town with one thriving industry, the preparations of scents and perfumes, the distilling of essences and oils to supply the world.

The basic materials for the perfumes of the far east, the near east, Europe, America, in fact the entire world are distilled and shipped from this delightful little town. A perfume such as Chypre. which the majority believe, is some magic concoction, possibly only in the laud of the oriental-eye, is manufactured here and extracted from the moss of the oak found in the neighboring community.

All the flowers used in the industry are grown within a radius of twenty-five miles of Grasse which furnishes a slight idea of the beauty of the country. It is one of the most charming spots on the Rivera. An atmosphere of poetry and sweet fragrance pervades the town. It is an eventful day in a woman's life to visit there-see the distilleries, be sprayed with many varieties of perfumes and be helped to a decision on a personal selection by men with a century or two of experience behind them.

There is a man there whose official designation is "The Nose" he being, of the sixth generation in direct line from father to son, serving as "The Nose" from this particular house. So extraordinary is his sense of smell that any perfume, any combination of oils, herbs, essences, flowers, or spices may be submitted to him for analysis and he can tell to the last faint petal, every ingredient therein.

Jasmine absolute, is the pure extract of the jasmine flower, and the most expensive because it requires one million flowers to make a ton and one ton to produce one kilo of extract. Jasmine is used in every good perfume. It is never sold alone, however, except to women who must have the most expensive without pity for the nose of a passerby. Few, if any, perfumes sold as a single flower odor are really the order of a single flower. The jasmine you buy is a combination of jasmine, rose, jonquil, and tuberose. When you buy lilies of the valley perfume, instead of a perfume made from the small white flower alone you have a combination of lilies of the valley, jasmine, tuberose, a little jonquil and a drop of mignonette. There are not enough lilies of the valley in the world to supply the trade for a pure extract and besides the pure essence of any of the single flowers is not agreeable.

The art of making perfumes is the skill of blending. There are about ten flowers used in the perfume industry: Jasmine, tuberose, narcissus, jonquil, violet, mimosa, mignonette, rose, carnation, orange blossom and probably a couple more. Spices too, are used, and herbs, and even a touch of chamomile.

One perfume popular in hot countries, also used by professional dancers is a mixture of ambergris, rose, patchouli, elong-elong, musk and chamomile. The dancers apply this under the upper arm and on the legs. When they move, the effect is like a faint, pleasing incense. The same perfume is recommended for use on strong furs. Orange peel, lemon, the extract of peach and pineapple are also incorporated into perfumes, if "the nose" decides a fruit flavor is needed to perfect scent. Mimosa is described as the perfume for yourself, not your neighbor. The method of experts when they are asked by particular women to prescribe an individual and appropriate perfume for them is based on the theory that every individual, no matter how scrupulous as to bodily hygiene, has an odor peculiar to her own person, Medical and other authorities endorse this fact. The idea is to get a perfume that blends harmoniously with the individual odor. One of the big institutions in Grasse supplies narrow strips of blotting paper, the length and thickness of a lead pencil, which patrons are requested to wear under the arms at night. Onto these blotting pads is put the perfume that either the patron shows a definite preference for herself or one that is suggested by her advised, a man experienced in summing up personality, type, and coloring of the inquirer.

If the experiment proves an ill-advised choice it is continued until perfect harmony is obtained.

To offset odors peculiar to furs experiments are advised with the stronger perfumes containing spices, herbs and flowers, until one is attained that counteracts the odor of the fur. For ermine, white jasmine is said to be the best—for caraculs, Persian lamb astrakhan, and the general run of furs violet is used with the happiest results.

1. Lilac—Poiret grants the most refined odor.
2. Chypre—Odor one associates with the cafe girl.
3. Flowers from the forest are allotted to the wholesome, vital femme who fills her lungs on foot, not in motors.
4. Heavy oriental perfumes are to be used only by the girl with a dash of the orient in her dress and in her eyes.

For light blond-flat delicate odors are suggested such as jasmine, lily of the valley.

Brunette-carnation

Gray haired woman-lilac or violet

Red Head-a combination of rose, carnation with a touch of chypre for the sophisticated red head; a lighter odor for the more delicate Titian haired, perhaps a combination of jasmine, tuberose and mignonette.

Rose is not for the blonde.

General rules for types judged on color alone, however, are not the policy to follow. The fastidious woman must insist upon the personal harmony referred to and then, having mastered that she may apply individuality by mixing her own from several different bottles, her secret to be wrapped in the bosom of mystery and the pleasing sent that clings about her.
Tuesday is violet day-Wednesday is rose

Paris

The influence of Napoleon is still supreme in Paris. Everyone visits his tomb which rests beneath the splendid dome of the church of the Invalides, which towers 350 feet above the sarcophagus, hewn from a single block of Siberian porphyry wherein lies the dust of the greatest military genius of all the ages. This tomb rest in a circular crypt or well, twenty feet deep and the visitor looks down upon it from above, thus compelling all who would see it, to bow before the mortal remains of Napoleon.

Arc de Triumph, the largest and most magnificent arch of victory in existence. It celebrates Napoleon's victories. He commenced its erections and his genius selected the most commanding place in Paris for its erection, where one may stand at the end of the Champ-Elysees the most splendid drive and promenade in Paris and look for a mile and a half to the Place de la Concorde. No finer view of the kind can be seen elsewhere in the world, particularly at night with the bordering street lights all ablaze.

The Cathedral of Notre Dame, nearly 700 years old, all its christenings, weddings, coronations are forgotten or unmentioned other then the fact that Napoleon was crowned there as an emperor. During the revolution of 1793 this place of worship was converted by the mob into a "Temple of Reason" and the statue of a virgin was replaced by that of Liberty. A Greek temple of Philosophy was erected in the church and a ballet dancer—a harlot—represented the enthroned figure of Reason, receiving in state the worship of her votaries. Again it was Napoleon, after he had come into power who received the credit of again opening the building for religious worship. When we visit the Madelain one of the most beautiful edifies in Paris, we see again the influence of Napoleon. He began the building as a "Temple of Glory" wherein should be commemorated each year, the victories of Jena and Austerlitz. It is patterned after the Parthenon of Athens, the most perfect structure ever erected by the architects of Greece. Napoleon did not live to see it finished but the architectural design was carried out and instead of being used to commemorate military victories, it is the aristocratic church of Paris. Among the religious pictures of the church, Napoleon has not been forgotten for one of the most prominent of the paintings is one representing Napoleon receiving the crown from Pope Pius the VII

This church which is 354 feet long and 141 feet in breadth, has no windows, the light being received thru three round skylights in the roof. It is surrounded by 52 massive Corinthian columns representing the 52 weeks of the year.

The Louvre is the largest and the most valued museum of pictures in the world and for it Paris has to remember Napoleon. A considerable portion of its treasures consists of the booty of Napoleon—treasures of art that he stole from the countries he conquered and sent to Paris. The most valuable pictures in the gallery is "Murill's Immaculate Conception." That was stolen from Spain.

In Paris the pedestrian must look out for himself, if hit he must not seek damages for he will get none—Parisian law Rue de Lappe near the Bastille is the most depraved street in Paris, a short narrow strip filled with dance halls. Pemod a nauseous absinthe-like drink, is the favorite beverage.

The chasseur a young messenger attached to hotels, cafés and bars is an example of the occasional lapse in French morals and knows more of Parisian depravity then the most satiated boulevardier. He is in league with bagnios and peep shows from which he gets his percentage. He has the brightness of the alert American newsboy.

Strange all the newspaper vendors in Paris are old men and women and they speak English.

In the woods at Ville D' Avray, near Sevre and twenty minutes from Paris is the little chateau of Corot, the printer. It has been kept intact. The surroundings are beautiful.

As Paris is synonymous with dressmakers one can hardly jam that pluse of it up. The "first showing" at the dress-making salons takes on the pomp of an exclusive ball. Sometimes held at night with especially invited guests arriving at nine p.m. arrayed as though attending an opera. Cocktails, champagne and cordials are served with a buffet lunch. Music floats from an orchestra hidden behind palms. The finest establishments are in rambling old mansions with courts which once housed notables such as Talleyrand.

Dress making is one of the most profitable trades in Paris. One proprietor paid taxes on a profit of $1,800,000 last year. Callot sisters own the "Galleries Lafayette". Jeanne Lanvin Pastou, Lucien Lelong and a dozen others are millionaires. Manikins imported from America have given, Parisian manikins a better name, save for one tragic example. The Pairisian manikin has always been underpaid and being naturally beautiful she followed the easiest way. To the French sales woman in dress—making parlors every feeling gives way when it becomes a question of profit. They appear enraptured and coo foolishly in a sort of hysterical babble. All work is on a percentage basis and a big sale is a small fortune. It is the poor American husband sitting in a corner fiddling with his cane or hat while his wife falls prey to the blandishments, who pays for grand stairways, carpeted salons and other magnificent trappings. Yet he seems to enjoy it just the same. Someone has called American husbands good—humored saps.

Notre Dame Cathedral

Notre Dame Cathedral venerable in gray, old age was the scene of a new ecclesiastical achievement, on Tuesday, April 15, 1919 when seven thousand American soldiers were stirred in heart and soul by what they saw, felt, and heard while paying homage to the memorials of our Savior. They were extended the grace to kneel and kiss a piece of the true cross of Christ; to kiss the actual nail which penetrated the flesh of their Savior and to kiss the crown of the crown of thorns called the service of veneration of Sacred Relics.

Notre Dame was crowded to the doors. Many had their first glimpse of this renowned sanctuary, where saints have died and sinners been converted; whose walls, arches and stately carved columns have witnessed the most marvelous and historic scenes of centuries—a temple of worship teeming with the important epochs of eight hundred years. They were facing an altar before which kings have been baptized. Monarchs newly crowned, have walked in all their majesty, amidst the pomp and splendor of church and state ceremony.

Within this sacred sanctuary has been heard the lamentations of a nation in despair and the "Te Deum" of a multitude when France was victorious. Genius has found inspiration of story and song, poem and praise, in this stately pile of stone—the perfection and triumph of gothic art in architecture.

With the procession of Sacred Relics came the great climax of the day's ceremonials. Before the altar appeared priests and prelates, monsignor, acolytes—all headed by uniformed custodians of the relics. The procession was as a prayer in the sight of the kneeling and standing congregation. Large sheaves of palm carried by the acolytes afforded meditation on the triumphal journey of Jesus into Jerusalem, when the poor and the faithful publicly avowed him a Savior. As this journey of marchers progressed and the relics of the world's great tragedy appeared in sight, there were few Catholic hearts that did not bow low before Calvary. Parnell Egan, famous American tenor, sang "O Savior Hear Me" the scene was enthralling. Cardinal Anette walked with head bent low. The sustained silence was intense and sacred, broken only by the hymn. Unconsciously, men dropped to their knees. Many were in tears. In the presence of the Crown of Thorns they felt themselves at the foot of the cross before that memorable day when Pontius Pilate washed his hands, saying: "I am innocent of the blood of this just man." A sense of realization that their eyes were seeing the crown which penetrated the brow of Jesus, that this sacred relic was actually passing in procession around the pious emotion of the spectators. This wonderful treasure was brought to Paris during the reign of St. Louis who constructed the Church of La Sainte Chapelle in which to shelter it. How wonderful for American soldiers to see it after 1900 years!

In another crystal encasement, carriers bore a piece of the Holy Cross—about 7 inches long. It is in a wonderful state of preservation. The nail of the Passion was carried in procession by other bearers. It is 6 in. long, capped with heavy iron, and shaped from a thickness of half an inch to a sharp ugly point. It was given by Charlemagne and preserved until 1790 in the Cathedral of St. Denis.

The kissing of the Sacred Relics was granted the American soldiers 5,000 awaited turn. After the veneration, the Treasury of Notre Dame was opened and the soldiers were permitted to view the wonderful collection of historic jewels, vestments, and antiques presented by kings, popes, and monarchs of the world. Their eyes were dazzled by the many jeweled casements given at different times by nations as repositories for the Sacred Relics exhibited throughout the service. They saw the Missal of the Mass used on the marriage ceremony of Napoleon the III. The collection includes the chalice of Pope Pius VII, contributed to Notre Dame by Napoleon. First coronation robe and cushion on which the Crown rested when Napoleon I was crowned in Notre Dame; a crucifix of the thirteenth century contributed by the Duke of Norfolk, at one time owned by Thomas A. Beckett; the gold crosses of Pope Pius IX and a magnificent monstrance presented by Napoleon; the chalice used to administer Holy Communion to Marie Antoinette and Louis XVI, the morning of their execution in 1793; the monstrance given by Louis XVIII to Notre Dame, studded with diamonds, rubies, and pearls. The vestments worn by the Popes and the Bishops of Paris, and the great collection of cameos bearing the portraits of 238 different Popes to the time of Leo XIII.

Every period of parish history is shown in the drawers and compartments of the Notre Dame Treasury.

The cathedral of our Lady Of Notre Dame de Paris was begun in the eleventh century and completed in the Thirteenth Century, seven hundred years ago, those memorable stones have witnessed the enthusiasm of the Crusaders of old, kneeling down at the foot of the altar before they leave on their long journey to Palestine to free Jerusalem from the Turks. It is the very soul and spirit of France, it was the spirit of those religions, Catholic, democratic people of the Middle Ages that gave birth, life, and immortality to those splendid temples of the living Lord.

French Peasants

Peasants do not live on farms, land is too valuable for that. They cultivate every inch and live in their villages.

The housewife and daughters go out in fields with husband and sons. In the North during the war the fields were full of women and children. Family washing—women kneel on the banks of the river and wields a brush. In some instances of the more progressive villages, the task is made lighter by a laundry. The women kneel in little boxes of straw on a cement floor and work all day in pleasant companionship. They wash the linens of the town literally and orally. In Le Marais the washing platform was built out in the river several feet from shore, it had a protective top and women were lined up on all sides, in their respective boxes scrubbing clothes. I expect this was municipal. Le Marais is a large city, conditions naturally are somewhat different than those of a village.

To go back to little French farms—Father and family are up early, his teams fed and with a son or two perched on the broad backs of horses are on way to the fields. He must spread fertilizer, keep weeds down and tend his farm as a garden. In fact, some of the United States gardens are as large as French farms.

The French do not have labor—saving machinery and so what he raises is the product of hard labor. He goes to market with team hitched tandem to a high two-wheeled creaking cart. Apparently these clumsy vehicles are so heavy that the owner has not the heart to meke the horses pull him also. He leads them. In fields, when he has not enough horse power, he makes the family cow assist. Late in the evening when this day is ended with the aid of a windlass and bucket he has drawn water from the well, he is free to set forth and mingle with his fellow men. In summer he sits at little tables on the sidewalk, in winter he sits inside and talks of many things, perhaps the condition of grapes, cost of living, and always the taxes. He always walks in the road, since in smaller places there are no sidewalks except an occasional narrow ledge in front of some buildings. In winter there is a chalky mud that clings and in summer the mud has become white dust that no one seems to worry about except the housewife who has the home to keep clean. The woman is the family banker and sales are a matter of bargaining. She is very shrewd in many matters.

The newspaper walks around the village. It is the town crier. He beats on a shiny old drum, he has.

There are gendarm even in the remote districts. They are a part of the national police force distributed over the country. They live in barracks situated at convenient points, usually between two villages. In their spare time they work their gardens, polish their equipment, and look after their families. The families are important for each child born, while the father is in service means an increase in pay.

Smocks are worn over clothing to save wear and wooden shoes or sabots to save leather is common. It has advantages also since wooden shoes are left on the mat outside the house. Callers can tell whether members he wishes to see are in. They still drag fagots in from the woods to burn in fireplaces as they did in old baronial days. Over the fireplace women do their boiling and frying. The wood they use is dead branches and a stick three inches through is unusual. Much of the bread comes from the bakery. The big round loaves have holes through them and an arm inserted through to carry conveniently. They are never wrapped in paper as our baking loaves.

The beds are big, deep beds with a mountain of covers topped with a feather tick. Brooms are made of twigs which are salvaged from woodpiles. No one throws handles away—they are kept and used for years. Much sewing is done by the women and girls and their handiwork is beautifully done.

COMBINING BUSINESS AND PLEASURE: THE VILLAGE GOSSIP Attending to Her Spinning Wheel at the Roadside and Letting Nothing That Goes On Escape Her.

Lyons—is the home of silk manufacture. Mulberry trees are cultivated in every part of the city, the food of the silk worm.

Versailles

Versailles is quite a city, wide shoddy paved streets lead to the palace. The court before the castle is very spacious. A guard took us through the marvelous palace built by Louis the XIV. Here in June of 1919, the Peace Treaty was signed; and January 1871, the German Empire was founded.

The gardens are most beautiful. Flowers, statuary, fountains, lake and more flowers. Yew trees trimmed in many shapes, rose trees and arbors. The castle is built around and in front of the gardens. There is another castle built for the Queen of Louis XVI at a far corner of the gardens. You walk and walk and at the end of a long avenue of trees, seemingly into the heart of a woods—the combination of nature and the artificial, near the castle there are many lakes and statues and beyond the Temple of Love, where they say Marie Antoinette came to hear the music, is her model farm, her dairy where she made cheese and butter for her royal family. Here the vine-covered mill, the dairy, and Tower of Marlborough are especially picturesque.

*Pershing and his armies of grim-faced American youths
with their steady eyes and grim-set chins.*

*Artist depiction of American Doughboy standing over a
French buddy's grave.*

German propaganda.

Following are the correct insignias and a brief outline of activities of the Combat Divisions of the American Expeditionary Forces. Rewritten from "Stars and Stripes" on the occasion of General Pershing's visit to fort Worth to make handy reference for the interested in the history of the American Expeditionary Forces.

FIRST DIVISION—REGULAR ARMY

Arrived in France June 27, 1917. Sommeville Sector near Nancy, Oct. 21 to Nov. 21, 1917; Ansauville Sector, Jan. 15 to April 3, 1918; Cantigny Sector, April 25 to July 7, 1918 (Battle of Cantigny, May 28 to 30); Soissons Operation, July 18 to 24; Saizerais Sector, Aug. 7 to 24; St. Mihiel, Sept. 12 and 13; Argonne-Meuse, Oct. 1 to 12; Mouzon, Nov. 5 and 6; Sedan, Nov. 7 and 8; to Coblenz Nov. 17 to Dec. 15, 1918.

Prisoners captured; 165 officers, 6,864 men. Total advance against resistance, 51 kilometers.

SECOND DIVISION—REGULAR ARMY

Arrived in France Oct. 26, 1917. Verdun and Toul Sector, March 18 to May 14, 1918; Northwest of Chateau-Thierry (almost continuous fighting), May 13 to July 9; Marne Counter Offensive, July 18 to 20; Marbache Sector, Aug. 9 to 24; St. Mihiel, Sept. 9 to 16; Blanc Mont Sector, Sept. 30 to Oct. 9; Argonne-Meuse, Oct. 30 to Nov. 11, 1918.

Prisoners captured; 225 officers, 11,742 men. Guns captured: 343 artillery, 1,356 machine guns. Total advance, 60 kilometers.

THIRD DIVISION—REGULAR ARMY

Arrived in France April 1, 1918. Chateau-Thierry Sector, May 31 to July 30; St. Mihiel Sector (Corps Reserve), Sept. 10 to 14; Argonne-Meuse, Sept. 30 to Oct. 27; march on Rhine Nov. 14, 1918.

Prisoners captured; 51 officers, 2,202 men. Guns: 51 artillery, 1,500 machine guns. Total advance, 41 kilometers.

FOURTH DIVISION—REGULAR ARMY

Arrived in France May 17, 1918. Marne Counter Offensive, July 13 to 21 (with French army); Vesle Sector (continuous fighting), Aug. 2 to 12; St. Mihiel (in reserve), Sept. 6 to 13; Argonne-Meuse, Sept. 25 to Oct. 19, 1918.

Prisoners captured; 72 officers, 2,684 men. Guns; 44 artillery, 31 machine guns. Total advance, 24½ kilometers.

FIFTH DIVISION—REGULAR ARMY

Arrived in France, May 1, 1918. Anould Sector, June 15 to July 16; St. Die Sector, July 18 to Aug. 22; St. Mihiel, Sept. 11 to 17; Argonne-Meuse, Oct. 12 to 22; second time in, Oct. 27 to Nov. 14, 1918.

Prisoners captured; 48 officers, 2,357 men. Guns; 93 artillery, 592 machine guns. Total advance, 32 kilometers.

SIXTH DIVISION—REGULAR ARMY

Arrived in France July 22, 1918. Gerardmer Sector, Sept. 3 to Oct. 13; Argonne-Meuse (First Army Corps Reserve), Nov. 1, 1918.

SEVENTH DIVISION—REGULAR ARMY

Arrived in France Aug. 11, 1918. Lorraine Sector, Oct. 9 to 29, and Oct. 29 to Nov. 11, 1918.

Prisoners captured; 1 officer, 68 men, 23 machine guns. Total advance, ¾ kilometer.

TWENTY-SIXTH DIVISION
New England National Guard.

Arrived in France Dec. 5, 1917. Chemin-des-Dames Sector, Feb. 6 to March 21, 1918; LaReine and Boucq Sector, April 3 to June 23; Northwest of Chateau-Thierry, July 10 to 25; Rupt and Tryon Sector, Sept. 3 to Oct. 8 (St. Mihiel, Sept. 13 to 14); North of Verdun, Oct. 18 to Nov. 14, 1918.

Prisoners captured: 61 officers, 3,027 men. Guns: 16 artillery, 132 machine guns. Total advance, 37 kilometers.

TWENTY-SEVENTH DIVISION
New York National Guard.

Arrived in France May 10, 1918. East Poperinghe Line, Belgium, July 9 to Sept. 3; Dickebush Sector, Belgium, Aug. 24 to Sept. 3; Hindenburg Line, France, Sept. 24 to Oct. 1; Jonc de Mer Bridge, Oct. 18; St. Maurice River, Oct. 19 to 21, 1918.

Prisoners captured: 66 officers, 2,292 men. Total advance, 11 kilometers.

TWENTY-EIGHTH DIVISION
Pennsylvania National Guard.

Arrived in France May 18, 1918. Southeast of Chateau-Thierry, Corps Reserve, June 30 to July 21; Vesle Sector (almost continual fighting), Aug. 7 to Sept. 8; Argonne-Meuse, Sept. 28 to Oct. 9; Thiaucourt Sector, Oct. 16 to Nov. 11, 1918.

Prisoners captured: 10 officers, 911 men. Guns: 16 artillery, 68 machine guns. Total advance, 10 kilometers.

TWENTY-NINTH DIVISION
National Guard From Maryland, New Jersey, Delaware, Virginia and District of Columbis.

Arrived in France June 27, 1918. Center Sector, Alsace, July 25 to Sept. 23; Grand Montagne Sector, North of Verdun, Oct. 7 to 30, 1918.

Prisoners captured: 2,187 officers and men. Guns: 21 artillery, 250 machine guns. Total advance, 7 kilometers.

THIRTIETH DIVISION
National Guard of North and South Carolinas and Tennessee.

Arrived in France May 24, 1918. Canal Sector, south of Ypres (with British), July 16 to Aug. 17; under U. S. command, Aug. 17 to Sept. 4; Gowy-Nauroy Sector, Sept. 22 to Oct. 2; Beaurevoir Sector, Oct. 3 to 12; Le Cateau Sector, Oct. 16 to 20, 1918.

Prisoners captured: 93 officers, 3,756 men. Guns: 81 artillery, 426 machine guns. Total advance, 29½ kilometers.

THIRTY-SECOND DIVISION
National Guard of Michigan and Wisconsin.

Arrived in France, Feb. 20, 1918. Alsace Front, May 18 to July 21; Fismes Front, July 30 to Aug. 7; Soissons Front, Aug. 28 to Sept. 2; Argonne-Meuse, Sept. 30 to Oct. 20; Dun-sur-Meuse, Nov. 8 to 11, 1918. Prisoners captured: 40 officers, 2,113 men. Guns: 21 artillery, 130 machine guns. Total advance, 56 kilometers.

THIRTY-THIRD DIVISION
National Guard of Illinois and West Virginia.

Arrived in France, May 24, 1918. Amiens Sector with Australians, July 21 to Aug. 18; Verdun Sector, Sept. 9 to Oct. 17; St. Mihiel Sector, Nov. 7 to 11, 1918.

Prisoners captured: 65 officers, 3,923 men. Guns: 92 artillery, 414 machine guns. Total advance, 36 kilometers.

THIRTY-FOURTH DIVISION

National Guard of Iowa, Minnesota, Nebraska and North Dakota.

THIRTY-FIFTH DIVISION

National Guard of Missouri and Kansas.

Arrived in France, May 11, 1918. North Sector of Wesserling Front (Vosges), July 1 to Aug. 14; Gerardmer South west Sector, Aug. 14 to Sept. 2; Argonne-Meuse, Sept. 21 to Oct. 1; Somme-Dieue Sector, Oct. 18 to Nov. 1, 1918.

Prisoners captured: 11 officers, 766 men. Guns: 24 artillery; 85 machine guns. Total advance, 12½ kilometers.

THIRTY-SEVENTH DIVISION

Ohio National Guard.

Arrived in France, June 22, 1918. Baccarat Sector, Aug. 4 to Sept. 6; Argonne-Meuse, Sept. 24 to Oct. 1; St. Mihiel Sector, Oct. 7 to 16; Lys and Escaut Rivers (Flanders), Oct. 31 to Nov. 4; Belgium, Ypres Sector, Nov. 7 to 11, 1918.

Prisoners captured: 22 officers, 1,462 men. Guns: 29 artillery, 361 machine guns. Total advance, 20 ½–3 kilometers.

FORTY-SECOND—RAINBOW DIVISION

National Guard of 26 States and District of Columbia.

Arrived in France, Nov. 1, 1917. Luneville, St. Clement-Baccarat Sector, Feb. 21 to March 23, 1918 (Under French Eighth and Seventh Army Corps). Baccarat Sector, March 31 to June 21; Souain and Esperance Sector, July 4 to 17; Trugny and Beauvardes, July 25 to Aug. 3 (Front of Fourth Army Corps on the Aisneuville, Essey and Pannes-de-Pannes (St. Mihiel Sector), Sept. 12 to 30; Georges-Cote de Chatillon (Argonne-Meuse), Oct. 13 to 31; south of Sedan, Nov. 4 to 10, 1918.

Prisoners captured: 14 officers, 1,201 men. Guns: 35 artillery, 408 machine guns. Total advance, 55 kilometers.

SEVENTY-SEVENTH DIVISION

National Army of New York City.

Arrived in France, April 13, 1918. Baccarat Sector, June 24 to Aug. 4; Fismes-Bazoches Sector, on Vesle Front, Aug. 12 to Sept. 16; La Harazee-Four de Paris-la Ville Marie Line, Sept. 26 to Oct. 16; Champig-Maulan Line, Aire-Meuse, Oct. 31 to Nov. 10, 1918.

Prisoners captured: 13 officers, 737 men. Guns: 44 artillery, 323 machine guns.

EIGHTIETH DIVISION

National Army of Virginia, West Virginia and Pennsylvania.

Arrived in France, May 30, 1918. Arras, July 23 to Aug. 18 (under British); St. Mihiel Salient, Sept. 12 to 16; Rethincourt Sector, Sept. 26 to 30 (Argonne); Mamnibois (Argonne), Oct. 4 to 12; St. Juvin (Argonne), Nov. 1 to 6, 1918.

Prisoners captured: 100 officers, 1,813 men. Guns: 13 artillery, 641 machine guns. Total advance, 57 kilometers.

EIGHTY-FIRST DIVISION

National Army of North and South Carolinas, Florida and Porto Rico.

Arrived in France, Aug. 16, 1918. East of St. Die and Sanet I' Etape Sector, Vosges, Sept. 18 to Oct. 19; Sommedieue Sector, Nov. 7 to 11, 1918.

Total advance, 4 1–2 kilometers.

EIGHTY-SECOND DIVISION

National Army of Georgia, Alabama and Tennessee.

EIGHTY-EIGHTH DIVISION

National Army of North Dakota, Minnesota, Iowa and Illinois.

NINETY-FIRST DIVISION

National Army of Alaska, Washington, Oregon, California, Idaho, Nevada, Montana, Wyoming and Utah.

NINETY-SECOND DIVISION

Traditional Indian Name for Negroes, The Buffalo Division National Army.

Total advance, 8 kilometers.

90th Division

NATIONAL ARMY OF TEXAS AND OKLAHOMA.

36th Division

NATIONAL GUARD OF TEXAS AND OKLAHOMA.

¶ It is written of the spoils of war: "The part of them that go down to battle shall be as the part of them that tarry; they shall share alike."

¶ Yet, no man who wears on his sleeve the badge of Overseas Service, can share with those left behind, his high honor. For he has been where men have been; where it was said: "At night the troubled earth beneath the lines was carpeted with pain; where death rode whistling in every wind; and the very mists were charged with torment; where of all things, spent and squandered, their precious life was held less dear."

¶ No man can share the honor, the glory and the tears for which that badge on his sleeve is the serviceable token.

¶ But he does share equally with you the responsibility f o r brave citizenship—shares a l i k e with all of you, who having not the badge of the soldier, are yet citizen-soldiers—men militantly loving right and justice, hating personal extravagance, political corruption and the red evils of the time; men consecrated to hard, good work and the high thinking that will keep America great and free.

*Y*ESTERDAY, as we write, was Armistice Day. As you read, the Birthday of Christ is near. These days should be considered together, for on them, as no other time during the year, the world is thinking in unison: of the hope of ending war, of the surety of the spreading of the gospel of peace.

Two types of men spoke yesterday, and the very skies were full of their exhortations. "It must not be again! O God, it must not be again! The dead themselves forbid it!" was the burden of the pleas uttered by the vast majority of the speakers. But the air carried this warning, too: "It will be again, unless we are ready. We must prepare for war; there is no other way to end it. We must keep faith with the living."

And both were right. It must not be again, but it will be again if some nation thinks it can make war pay. The lessons war teaches—that even victory is defeat, that indemnities never repay, that disease, distress, and death ride under the most victorious banners—these lessons are all easily forgotten. War will never end merely because it is brutal.

We must seek a more compelling motive, find a more cogent reason. Some would see the motive in the growth of brotherly love; others would find the reason in an increase of battlements. Experience sides with the latter: no nation has yet loved another too much to fight with it, but many a nation has refrained from calling out its legions because another could muster more men-at-arms. Self-interest still rules supreme, and prudence, more often than right, has a place at the council table.

Nora Elizabeth Daly (Posthumously)

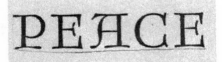

PEACE

How, then, can the nations be made to furl their battle-flags forever-more? We wish we knew. There is no single cure for war—none, that is, that all the nations will accept. And yet there is not one that does not know that war never pays and will pay less, and cost more, as science perfects the possibility of murdering a city in a night. Contemplating that fact of the future, how can one refrain from crying, "It must not be again"?

And as it must not, so it need not. The Christmastide tells us that. He whose birth we celebrate was quick to resent wrong, slow to offend. The manhood of the Christ would have taken him into the world's struggle against blatant autocracy, but it would have kept him from being the aggressor. Might not following him bring the world to peace?

May it be for the world a Happy New Year!

WILLIAM FREDERICK BIGELOW, EDITOR

Here also was the great salvage dept. No. 8, where in the fall of 1918, nearly a thousand American officers and soldiers, seven hundred and fifty French civilians and over five thousand French women were engaged in making fit for service once more millions of dollars worth of salvaged army clothing.

a peasant is shown tilling a
battle-scarred field, plowing up now
and then a rifle, a shell or a strand
of barbed wire.

A peasant is shown tilling a battle-scarred field, plowing up now and then a rifle, a shell or a strand of barbed wire.

Signal Corps telephone and telegraph station in a cellar in Château-Thierry.

Brigadier General Dennis E. Nolan, Chief Intelligence Office of the A.E.F. has somewhere written that the basics of combat intelligence is the Intelligence Personnel with line troops.

The aim of Intelligence is to describe the enemy's focuses, determine the location of his units, discover his intentions and when and where he will carry them out. One must be able to read and decode them first of all, however, these messages must be picked off the enemy's wires—the job of the radio operators sitting under shell fire and gas, squatting in muddy trenches concealed but not protected in the water-filled cellars of ruined houses, cold wet and hungry but always attentive. It was monotonous, not much thrill of accomplishment. They did not understand the enemy cipher but they must get them accurately and forward to G.H.Q. The man at the rear is entirely dependent on the operator—a letter lost may be the key to the puzzle.

Chaumont-Haute-Marne, once the seat of General Headquarters of the A.E.F. in the valley of the Marne, a little hilltop city, the Suize River a part of it with fluffy little basket willows that define its course.

Perhaps next to the Franco—American monument is a new wonder Grotte de Norte Dame de Lourdes." It is a faithful duplicate of the original, "the famous shrine of the Pyrenees." It is said to have been built by some wealthy individual in fulfillment of a vow that if he lived through the perils of the war he would establish at Chaumont this copy of the miraculous grotto. It is situated out on the edge of the Faubourg de Lanneries, close to the Suize and at the foot of the slope where the road climbs out of the valley and runs off in the direction of the Bar-sur-aube and Paris.

One phase of the A.E.F. occupation and a most interesting one—"The Glass House" in the barracks grounds at the American—G.H.Q. It was an interesting group of new-style soldiers. The Glass House was a mystery place to the several hundred other officers of General Perishing's headquarters staff. It stood by itself in an obscure but out-of-the-way location. Behind one of the main barracks buildings and near the low-lying sheds that housed the commissary stores. It was a one-story shack of concrete and glass.

Out of the beaten path it may not be easily recalled by most of the men stationed at Chaumont. At the period of greatest expansion of the A.E.F this obscure building housed a staff of seventy-two officers and men. They were members of the Code and Cipher Section, Intelligence Division, General Staff; called in army colloquialism "G2-A6." The chief was a Regular Army officer—practically all the others were temporary officers gathered from all branches of the military service and from the most diverse civil callings. Their job at GHQ was to decipher the German code messages picked up along the front by Signal Corps operators. Strangely enough, scarcely any of these code experts possessed any knowledge of codes before entering the army. They were selected on the showing entered on their qualification cards because of their pursuit in civil life of unusual hobbies. The fundamental requisite of course, was that all of them must understand the German language. Beyond that they need little else in common. An infantry officer was chosen because his qualification card showed that, although a lawyer by profession, he had made considerable outside study in archeology. Another man was taken because he was a Chess expert. An architect was shown by his card to have devoted years to self-imposed task of studying Hebrew, Persian and other Oriental languages. All had given proof of studious habits mired in the pursuit of information that demanded close application and logical methods of thought. Almost without exception, the officers so chosen proved able code experts.

This hand picked crowd was confined in the glass house, after one or two discretions of conversation had reveled the necessity of preventing the kind of information they handled being made the subject of office gossip about headquarters. For the same reasons, the code experts formed a separate mess of their own and after they lived an almost monastic life, associating only infrequently with the other officers. Their section operated day and night. The German signal wires hummed twenty-four hours a day with messages along the front. This meant that our own signal corps radio operators must be listening at their sets every hour of the twenty-four, writing down cabalistic communications that passed between the enemy ports. From the front these reports were telegraphed to Chaumont and turned over to the Code and Cipher Section for translation.

Opposite

There is one spot which no American if he ever visit Chaumont would consciously neglect. Beside the road just in front of St. Aignan's chapel is the site of the American Cemetery, which lay something like two years beside the older French parish cemetery.

The weeds and rough grass now cloaking the upheaved ground sloping down to the Marne would hardly betray to a stranger that here had been the resting place of the bodies of hundreds of brave men, most of whom died in Base Hospital No.15, until they were removed for return to the United States for final interment in one of our permanent cemeteries in France. But with the fine delicacy of feeling, so often shown by them in such matters, the French have commemorated the fact for years to come in the dignified monument beside Neuf Chateau road which bears on its face, side by side, the Coats of Arms of the United States and of Chaumont and the legend in French:

"1917-1921. This simple stone will recall to future generations that here has been a cemetery containing the bodies of more then six hundred American soldiers who fought at our sides for right and liberty." Such expressions of feeling as this go deeper than surface courtesy. They come from hearts of the people.

On a conspicuous site opposite the Boulingas Park with the dark masses of trees along the Boulevard Gambetta as a background is an expressive symbol of Franco-American friendship. The arriving American soldiers receiving the cordial handclasp of the

Spirit of France as she stands with her other arm resting maternally over the shoulder of her own war-worn poilu, is a faithful type of the energetic clean-cut doughboy who composed the backbone of the A.E.F. Though dedicated by the then President of France M. Poincare with the assistance of an impressive assemblage of French and American dignitaries, civil and military, the cost of the monument was defrayed entirely by a popular subscription to which every town in the department of the Haute-Marne contributed, the largest part being raised by or in Chaumont itself. It is a good thing that such a memorial to American General Headquarters has been raised, for already oblivion has over taken most of the once overwhelming evidences of our occupation of Chaumont. The big entertainment hut and the rambling officer's Y.M.C.A. building is devoted exclusively to dust and mud, depending on the weather Caserne Damremont seems silent compared to the buzzing hives of American G.H.Q.

Neuf Château

After starting from Chaumont toward the St. Mihiel front, a run of about twelve miles in the direction of Neuf Chateau is a little village with the sign "Treaty of Andelot was signed in 587." I may know more about the treaty someday.

However, Andeleot was noted among the Americans for its crooked crazy streets, only a mile or two beyond Rimaucourt, a sharp bend in the road a double row of shapely trees and beyond the crest of hill 260. This spreading barracks of a base hospital once covered the gentle southward slope between the road and the little Sueur River. Rimaucourt cared for its full share of the hundred and ninety thousand members of the A.E.F., who at one time were occupying beds in American hospitals, most of them as a result of battle wounds or of the influenza epidemic. Five or six miles further on at Lafauche there are no remains of the Advance Shell Shock Hospital. A mile or so from Lafauche between Liffol-le-Petit and from Liffol-le-Grande is still to be found something of the vast spread of the trackage of the American advance. Regulating stations, whose warehouses and barracks and long strips of freight cars once transformed the whole countryside. Along the railroad extending from Bologne to Neuf Chateau are still some of the sidetracks of massive American steel and switches and some evidence of the narrow gauge.

The road from Chaumont enters a wide street Rue Neuf Chateau now called Rue President Wilson beyond to the right merges the Commissary road. Weather-beaten, wooden signs bear

"Language-Belfort" and "Taul-Novey-Espinol." First American army had its headquarters at Neuf Chateau. The road to Langres, is Bazoilles, one time the center of vast American base hospital installations and American visiting gatekeeper (trains) at Bazoilles after the war. They were left to believe, that the American Occupation, they clearly esteemed as its day of greatest glory. It must have been a busy place for no less than eight base hospitals were concentrated there with many thousands of beds, a large number of them occupied during the Battle of the Meuse-Argonne. The gatekeeper receives small pay of six hundred francs a year. Its advantages are the use of the rent-free house and the privilege of cultivating as much ground on the railroad right of way in garden stuff as the family can care for.

The statue of Jeanne d'Arc in the Place Jeanne d'Arc, Neufchateau

The statue of Jeanne d' Arc the heroine clasping her banner—a reminder that once as a little girl she accompanied her parents and brothers and sister to Neuf Chateau when they were obliged to flee from Domremy, a few miles north, before a raid of the Burgundian allies of the English, a little further on is fine old 11th century church of St. Nicholas looking down from the sluggish waters of the Morizon.

Douremy—la—Pricella, where more than 500 years ago, there was born and lived for a period of seventeen years, a little girl, daughter of family of farmers, who gave to France and to the world the most glorious tradition of unselfishness, chivalry, and pure devotion to God and native land that is recorded in history—Jeanne d' Arc, of course. Thousands of and tens of thousands of American soldiers made the pilgrimage to Domremy—where they viewed with curiosity and deep interest the humble house, the church close beside it and the ambling village. Since Domremy is only about seven miles north of Neuf Chateau and on the main road between that place and Commercy and the best road to Gondrecourt and Colombey-les-Belles also branch off near there, it was centrally located in relation to the scene of American activities. In 1918, French and American flags were draped together about Jeanne's Alter in the village church, wherein stands the massive stone font in which she was baptized. On national holidays now the "Stars and Stripes" is raised in its old place beside the Tricolor.

In 1918, when one headed out of Neuf Chateau toward the Salient he had the choice of two roads for reaching Taul, which was ordinanily, the last stop before proceeding northward. When in the vicinity of Limey one is presented with immovable obstacles to impede their progress in the direction of Metz or later on after the 1st American Army had shoved obstacles back to the neighborhoods of Vandieres and Rembercourt and Haumont. How different today is the scene—once a desolate waste of shell holes, now fields of alfalfa—the fresh stuccoed walls, and bright new red—tile roofs of the restored village. The cattle browsing peacefully in green pastures of what had been "No Man's Land. In a spot between Seicheprey and Flirey the skeletons of five or six Americans were found—the people at the American cemetery were notified and remains had proper burial in one of the permanent American cemeteries.

Colombey-les-Belles the immense landing fields and the wide spreading hangars and construction and repair shops of the advance Section Air Service assembly and repair depot another road from Neuf Chateau another Domreruy and Vacouleurs—eastward then Bois de Domgermain to Bleurod and north into Taul.

All over this country in the vicinity of Gondrecourt and Abaiuville, and up the roads towards Taul and Commercy and Bar-le-Due are scores of villages, each of which had its contingent of billeted Yanks at one time or another. Vaucouleurs, once seat of a Pursuit Group Airborne, above whose streets a large statue of Jeanne d' Arc now looks out over the valley from the peak of the still unfinished memorial church on the site of the ancient Chateau.

The highland between the valleys of the Ornain and the Meuse one village breaks the monotony—Vouthon the birthplace of Jeanne d' Arc's mother Isabelle Romee and in going westward, when one comes out of the forest a few kilometers from Gondrecourt, he sees to the north the vast panorama of open and uninhabited country in the "Grand Valley."

The church at Domremy from the bridge across the Meuse. The d'Arc cottage, Jeanne's birthplace, is behind the trees at the right

For two and a half years army transports unloaded laden caskets at Hoboken; caskets containing the remains of 45,000 of the A.E.F. dead. Only bodies requested by relatives were returned. The last body arriving in February of 1922. In every instance the prayers were read by an army Chaplin of the Protestant faith and of the Catholic faith and by a former Chaplin of the Jewish faith.

The soldier dead may sleep under the shade of American trees and shrubs according to present plans. A laboratory is maintained in Paris for carrying on experiments in soil and arboriculture to determine whether elms and oaks and American native shrubs can be successfully maintained in the foreign soils. This is probably completed by now.

When the work of identifying and honoring the dead of the A.E.F. is compared with that of the other allied armies it is discovered that the Americans have succeeded in a most remarkable way. Only 2,000, less than 2 per cent, of our dead remain unidentified. In the French and British Armies from 40 to 50 percent.

Graves are leveled to the surface and sodded at the head of each, an identical headstone for officers and enlisted men standing 24 by 13 inches above ground, bearing the fallen soldier's name in full, his state, his rank regiment, and division, and date of death. Space is left at bottom for biblical or other appropriate text if the family desires it. Inserted above the name there will appear for Gentiles, a Latin cross and for Jews the double star of David. No departure from the regulation and size of the headstone will be permitted in any case. Central plaza, a flag pole will fly the Stars and Stripes and so long as civilized notions endure it will wave in the breeze above the American dead.

The American Flag is still in Europe, it floats over eight cemeteries, six in France, one in Belgium, and one in England. this map shows where American troops are in their last bivouac on French, Belgian and English soil.

WHERE AMERICANS LIE "IN FLANDERS FIELDS"
Men from the United States, 365 in all, are gathered here at
Waereghem, Belgium, beneath their flag.

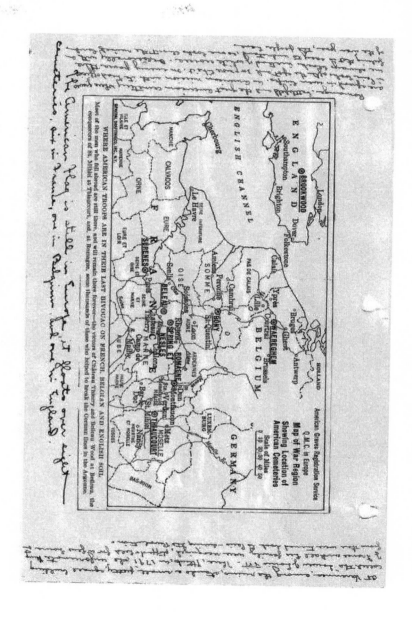

A German writer, Paris correspondent of the Berliner Tageblatt, a sympathetic observer of the destruction wrought by his countrymen in Northern France tells of part of his trip thru that territory. He says the guide relates in a matter of fact way that of the 121 villages which he covers on his trip, some eighty have been utterly destroyed. This part of the journey from Clermont en Argonne to Bourneville, has all been wrecked by the war, but the worst came after he reached Varenner. From there to Verdun it is a desert—over which the horsemen of the apocalypse have swept. At only one point is there any evidence of restoration, and this has become one of the sights of the region—the American cemetery, St. Mihiel, at Romagne below Montfuaucon. Americans do things. On a gently rising hill it lies. Some kilometers before reaching this point are noted little white signboards along the road directing them to this gigantic graveyard. Many relatives of the fallen cross the sea to visit the last resting place of those dear to them. Within half a mile a field of white suddenly greets you, tombstones of equal size shining in the sunlight. Crosses for Protestants and Catholics and stars for Jews. Sad, indeed, as is the thought of a whole army of vigorous young boys here slumber in death, there is nothing gloomy about it. It is a bright and cheerful place. And the army of the dead has its commander an American officer and his staff reside in a group of tidy houses opposite the entrance to guard and care for the resting place of their dead countrymen.

Outside the entrance of Aisne-Marne Cemetery, is a circular flower bed beautiful with flowers and in its center and on either side is German Carrum. In center of cemetery on a tall white pole hangs an American flag. There are no flowers planted within this cemetery and the white crosses stand in this instant back to back in rows across level green sod, which is separated into sections by gravel walks. Names of soldiers and company they belong to are only inscriptions on crosses. Some instances, "unknown soldier".

Chance falling of a shell decided sites of battlefield cemeteries that are scattered throughout the combat area over which the American forces fought. For instance during the July fighting in the Chateau—Thierry Salient a German H.E., fell near the village of Torcy killing 23 Americans, two Frenchmen who were interred in the crater formed by the explosion. The following September the shell hole was filled up and smoothed over the dead were ranked in regular rows of graves and the place became officially known as Cemetery no. 64.

Permanent National Cemeteries for Dead in Europe

Suresnes near Paris—1,491

Meuse Argonne at Romagne—14,123 (who broke the German lines in the Argonne)

Aisne—Marne at Belleau Wood—2,438 (fought in Belleu Wood at Chateau Thieny)

Somme at Borny—1,900 (nearly 2,000 of the 27th division)

St. Mihiel at Harcourt—4, 258 (those who took part in St. Mihiel defensive)

Oise-Aisne, at Seringes at Nesles—6, 143

Warrengham, Belgium—450 (In Flanders field)

Brookwood, England—699 (graves of men who died in transport, sinkings, or in hospitals.)

Second Lieutenant
J. Hunter Wickersham, M.H.

THIS poem, here published for the first time, was written by Lieut. J. Hunter Wickersham, 353rd Infantry, Eighty-ninth Division, on the eve of the St. Mihiel attack, and was enclosed in his last letter to his mother, Mrs. Mary E. Damon, of Denver, Col. Lieutenant Wickersham was killed on the following day, September 12, 1918, near Limey, in an exploit which won for him the posthumous award of the Congressional Medal of Honor. His citation reads:

"Advancing with his platoon during the St. Mihiel offensive, he was severely wounded in four places by the bursting of a high-explosive shell. Before receiving any aid for himself he dressed the wounds of his orderly, who was wounded at the same time. He then ordered and accompanied the further advance of his platoon, though weakened by the loss of blood. His right hand and arm, being disabled by wounds, he continued to fire his revolver with his left hand until, exhausted by loss of blood, he fell and died from his wounds before aid could be administered."

The Raindrops on Your Old Tin Hat

The mist hangs low and quiet on a ragged line of hills,
  There's a whispering of wind across the flat.
You'd be feeling kind of lonesome if it wasn't for one thing—
  The patter of the raindrops on your old tin hat.

An' you just can't help a-figuring—sitting there alone—
  About this war and hero stuff and that,
And you wonder if they haven't sort of got things twisted up,
  While the rain keeps up its patter on your old tin hat.

When you step off with the outfit to do your little bit
  You're simply doing what you're s'posed to do—
And you don't take time to figure what you gain or lose—
  It's the spirit of the game that brings you through.

But back at home she's waiting, writing cheerful little notes,
  And every night she offers up a prayer
And just keeps on a-hoping that her soldier boy is safe—
  The Mother of the boy who's over there.

And, fellows, she's the hero of this great big ugly war,
  And her prayer is on the wind across the flat,
And don't you reckon maybe it's her tears, and not the rain,
  That's keeping up the patter on your old tin hat?

The Story of "Rouge Bouquet"

In a letter to his wife May 4-18 Joyce Kilmer said,

There is to be an American banquet at our house one day the day when I exhibit to myself correnda the glory of my life. Yourself. Journal like them all— Watson a gifted artist from Richmond & who is now at work on a fine drawing which must accompany Rouge Bouquet.

Bob Lee, Titterton (my especial friend), Beck, Mott, Kerrigan, Levinson—say a prayer for them all, they're brave men and good, and splendid company. . . . Jongberg is up here for a brief spell; he is a Swedish-Irishman, and now he is posing for St. Michael for Watson, using a bayonet for a sword. Levinson (in full uniform, including belt and helmet) is being model for the soldiers leaving Rouge Bouquet for Heaven. He is a quaint little French-Jewish-American, with whom we have a lot of fun. They all trooped into the room where Titterton and I sit writing to our respective sweethearts, to ask about the style of St. Michael's sword and that of his halo. These questions settled, Watson became enamored of the idea of angels saluting, and devised a whole manual of arms for angels—as "Angels, attention! Wings raised, by the numbers. 1 up! 2 down! Wings flap! Hey you down there! What's the matter with you? Don't you know enough to keep your hands down when you flap your wings? Awkward squad for you to-morrow!" Then they went back to their work.

A week later, on June 1st, within a month of his death, Kilmer wrote his wife:

I have interesting things to do. . . . To mail you this letter and a splendid drawing for "Rouge Bouquet," by Emmett Watson, of ours.

The drawing was duly mailed—and never received. "Rouge Bouquet" appeared in *Scribner's Magazine* without it. Nearly five years have passed, and even Mr. Watson, himself quite aware, from experience, of the delays that vex the postal systems of the best-regulated armies, has about given up hope for it. He therefore consented to redraw it from memory for The American Legion Weekly, remembering the original so well that he has been able virtually to duplicate it.

"Rouge Bouquet" was written in memory of nineteen members of Company E, 165th Infantry, killed when a minnenwerfer shell struck a front-line dugout on March 7, 1918, in "a wood they call the Rouge Bouquet," Rocroi, Forêt de Parroy, Lunéville sector. On St. Patrick's Day, ten days later, the Rev. Fr. Francis P. Duffy, chaplain of the 165th, read the poem at special services held behind the lines, while a bugle played Taps in a neighboring wood.

Joyce Kilmer was killed during the fierce struggle of the Rainbow Division for the heights north of the river Ourcq. He was leading a patrol sent out to locate a group of troublesome machine guns. When the infantry advanced a little later they found him lying on the ground, apparently looking intently ahead. They called to him. There was no answer. A German bullet had pierced his brain. He had volunteered his services to the major commanding the front-line battalion because his own battalion was not to be in the lead that day.

Sergeant Kilmer is buried in the American cemetery at Fère-en-Tardenois, barely a hundred yards from the spot where he fell. His is one of the 32,000 American graves in Europe.

CRÉCY-AU-MONT, May 28, 1922. "Offerte à l'église de Crécy-au-Mont en souvenir de JOYCE KILMER. Mort pour la patrie." Donor, Poetry Society of America.

[handwritten note, partially illegible]
One of the most beautiful and appropriate tributes to American soldiers who gave their lives in the war is the church bells given in their memory — the devastated regions of France, when the American war sought a tone bell was placed with messages telling in the fate of the government, bought scrap of the precious metal was sent into giving the metal down for munitions. The above clipping refers to a bell in honor of Kilmer.

Rouge Bouquet

By Joyce Kilmer

IN a wood they call the Rouge Bouquet
  There is a new-made grave today,
Built by never a spade nor pick
Yet covered with earth ten meters thick.
There lie many fighting men,
  Dead in their youthful prime,
  Never to laugh nor love again
  Nor taste the summertime.
For Death came flying through the air
And stopped his flight at the dugout stair,
Touched his prey and left them there,
  Clay to clay.
He hid their bodies stealthily
In the soil of the land they fought to free
  And fled away.
Now over no grave abrupt and clear
  Three . . . .
And per . . . . . . ave young spirits hear
  The . . . .
"Go to sleep!
Go to sleep!
Slumber well where the shell screamed and fell.
Let your rifles rest on the muddy floor,
You will not need them any more.
Danger's past;
Now at last,
Go to sleep!"

THERE is on earth no worthier grave
  To hold the bodies of the brave
Than this place of pain and pride
Where they nobly fought and nobly died.
Never fear but in the skies
Saints and angels stand
  Smiling with their holy eyes
    On this new-come band.
St. Michael's sword darts through the air
And touches the aureole on his hair
As he sees them stand saluting there,
  His stalwart sons;
And Patrick, Brigid, Columkill
Rejoice that in veins of warriors still
  The Gael's blood runs.
And up to Heaven's doorway floats,
  From the wood called Rouge Bouquet,
A delicate cloud of buglenotes
  That softly say:
"Farewell!
Farewell!
Comrades true, born anew, peace to you!
Your souls shall be where the heroes are
And your memory shine like the morning star.
Brave and dear,
Shield us here.
Farewell!"

Copyright, 1918, by George H. Doran Company

U.S. entered the World War on April 6, 1917. The first American soldiers in Europe were not an Army Corp of infantrymen but a medical detachment base hospital #4 one of hundred and fifty men, fifty nurses, a score of physicians and surgeons, commanded by a regular army colonel, a veteran of the Philippines and five regular army sergeants, left New York on May the 8th and landed in Liverpool May 18, 1917.

Nurses and medical men went on to London, where they were to be received by the King and Queen and the recruits to the coast resort town of Blackpool. On May 25th they crossed the English Channel up one hundred miles of the winding River Seine between La Harve and Rouen and at Rouen in the heart of Normandy, the first American set forth on French soil. At a hospital camp on the edge of a sandy plain, where Napoleon had trained his soldiers in another World War more than a century before, the first American flag that had been carried overseas was raised and there it had been flying for weeks. When General Pershing and the first combat troops landed at St. Nazaire.

Lest I forget, I must write down here a tribute paid to the medical department by one of the big men of the war. He includes the men only—of course nurses did not go beyond the line, although in danger, those who were with hospitals just back of the lines by bombing. The officers and the men of the medical department who go up and beyond the firing line to aid and carry away their fellow comrades are subjected to all risks and dangers without an opportunity to hit back; the men in the train who carry food, ammunition, clothing, and supplies through shell and machine gun fire risking life and limb a task doubly hazardous because carried out in the dark more often than in daytime, are as much combatants of a combat division as of the men on the line who have at least the satisfaction of hitting back.

First Shot in the World War

A battered old soixante—quinze gun that still wears the war paint of its combat days in France has found a resting place of honor at the United States Military Academy at West Point with other relics that remind the youthful warriors in Uncle Sam's national school of the gallant deeds their predecessors have preformed in all the wars in the Republic's history. A plate on the gun informs the world that it is the gun with which Americans fired the first shot in the World War after our entry. This gun belonged to Battery C, Sixth field artillery First Division, and at the time the history—making shot was fired the battery was commanded by Captain Indus R. Mc Lendon. On the morning of October 23, 1917—battery C had just arrived in position in the Duneville sector, four hundred meters east of Bathlmont.

The first invasion after months of training in France had taken over a section of the front from the French and everybody in the division was keen to have a shot at the enemy. It does not appear that Battery C has any particular target to shoot at and there is lacking any clear explanation as to how the thing came about, but official records show that at 6:05 am, of Oct. 23rd the gun now at West Point was aimed in the general direction of Berlin and banged away with a shell that went screaming over to the Bosche outfits holding the St. Mihiel sector to notify them that a new enemy had appeared on the Western Front. Since our military traditions are carried on so largely there the graduates of the West Point Military

Academy, the old gun of Battery C, sixth artillery, is destined, no doubt, to bear through the years to come the honor of having fired the first shot of the war. But there was that other American shot fired much earlier in our participation.

The gun that fired the first shot for America in the World War, October 23, 1917. It was manned by men of C Battery, Sixth Field Artillery.

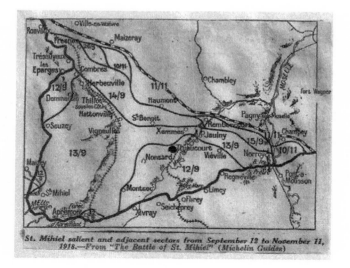

St. Mihiel salient and adjacent sectors from September 12 to November 11, 1918.—From "The Battle of St. Mihiel" (Michelin Guides)

Map showing World War I Meuse-Argonne Battle Sector
in 1918

September—26-1918 Offensive between Nesue River and Argonne
Forest

L.W.Suckert in Stars and Stripes
Here a rumble an a jumble
And a bumpkin an a thud
As I waken from my restless sleep
Here in my bed of mud
N C pull my blanket tighter
Underneath my shelter fly
As I listen to the thunder
O the trucks a-rolling by

The World War took a great deal out of the world. Men's lives,
lives of defenseless women and helpless children. It took health of
distorted normal bodies into vessels of agony. It burned and blew up
and sunk tens of billions of dollars worth of property.

War is torturing
Service to their country, open season to every American girl's
heart. No American girl could wish greater happiness have so
sacrificed themselves to the future.

Among jester appreciations is this: that the infantry is the army and
that all others services are mere auxiliaries.

Soiully was the old headquarters of the defense of Verdun.

Delita, Canopic and Magestic were three great ships in war.

Nora's personal thoughts from the time she left New York to her return home.

Friday Sept. 6, 1918—Rounsenalle and Duncan were over from "The Madison" this evening I was packing, parting in a few snaps and feeling down right blue. Seeing them helped a lot.

Sunday Sept. 8, 1918—I had a full day yesterday—John and Joseph came over from Camp Dix. Got to our hotel about 4:30 p.m. I sent a telegram to Camp Dix as soon as I received John's letter and he called long distance immediately. I was so afraid that they might not be able to come before I left. I was most awfully glad to see them, although it did make me feel somewhat lonely. They told me mama had been sick in bed and that Jule Daly was with her. How I wished I might be home for a little while. Saw the boys Saturday evening, then Laskin, Mueller and I went to confession at St. Ann's Church on 12th St. off 3rd Ave.—went to 6 o'clock mass this a.m., were late, so went back to 7 o'clock. John and Joseph came while we were at breakfast-said goodbye. Had a few tears, did try hard not to. Finished my breakfast, then Keach, Broseh, Larkin, Boutillier and I went for a bus ride. Wrote several cards after lunch, then Boutillier, Keach and I went to "The Little Church Around the Corner"—very quaint and unusual. After returning to Hotel I wrote a few more cards, finished just in time. Larkin and I were late for roll call we were to start for boat a 4 p.m. We were not a bit excited but I'll admit somewhat curious and slightly thrilled as to what came next. We walked to 4th Ave. two blocks from the "Irving" and from there walked down to 14th St. and took the "Crosstown" car to Hoboken side to the transportation dock, port or whatever it is called. We lined up in twos. A Red Cross man and woman gave to each of us, two cards and a telegram to be sent to relatives or friends, C.O.D. after the safe arrival of our boat "oversees". Each also received a package of cigarettes. I'd never smoked in my life. They informed us that mail from now on until war ended would need no stamps. I sent one card to John and Joseph and one to a friend—had written home before leaving hotel. After much waiting we were given our cabin tickets and walked up the gang plank to our boat, the Melita—a British boat and said to be best in the convoy. There are fourteen boats in convoy, several torpedoes, destroyers, a battleship, an airplane, a dirigible and an observation balloon which was attached to a destroyer. The balloon, airplane and dirigible and some of the destroyers returned after following us for some miles out. They are 2500 troops on board ship, and fifty nurses (30,000) troops in entire convoy and five hundred nurses. We had a wonderfully good dinner goose n' everything. After roll call, which was about 8:30, we found our suitcases and blanket rolls, they were taken to our cabins by the soldiers. I was very tired, so after a good face wash, went to bed and slept fine. No one is allowed on deck after seven, windows are closed and life belts worn constantly except at meal time and while sleeping.

Sept. 9, 1918—Monday—Rumor says we are bound for Liverpool, England. We left Anchorage about 8:00 o'clock—were at breakfast when we started, rather disliked seeing the New York shore line disappear. The Statue of Liberty was looked at with longing and hope of being seen again by many. It seemed wonderful to be sailing along so smoothly. We had a splendid lunch. I think we reached the ocean about 2 p.m. I was anticipating a wonderful trip with no sea-sickness but as we came in for dinner, I became desperately dizzy and ill and left the dinning room early. I will not dwell on how I felt but my unfounded sympathy goes to those who may have had similar experiences. Crombie, a Canadian nurse, whose brother was killed about a year ago and Edgar knew slightly at Camp Lewis, were my cabin mates both very fine. Our cabin windows are closed at dusk makes it rather close and stuffy. Wanted and tried to get up but the effort was to much.

September 11, 1918—Wednesday—Went on deck after having a glass of milk and a wafer, but couldn't stay. Makes me sick to look at anything or anybody and I would love to be on deck and enjoy everyone. I like people and I must hurry and feel better. Music, movies, dancing oh well I shall be thankful for each day gone and a safe arrival in France.

September 12, 1918—Thursday—Fourth day, my birthday, I feel better. The sunsets are beautiful, the most beautiful I've seen-and the moonlight—of all the exquisite pictures, each evening more impressive. The ocean, fascinating, mysterious-the world is lovely, why this war?

September 13, 1918—Friday—Was up on deck nearly all day Oh joy! Had lunch there, everyone is kind. In the p.m. had tea, nearly made me sick again, but went on deck the portside, where a good strong breeze had me feeling good in a short time. Went down for dinner, and don't think I shall eat again. The girls are sweet.

September 14, 1918—Saturday—Miss Washburn visit's the sick everyday-miserable, I am. Someone said we were about 600 miles from Newfoundland. Oily-rough sea, chilly. Before leaving, Lacoma, Roach and Splin, in good faith, said tomatoes were good for sea sickness. I had a can with me and tried them today-they at least tasted good. Tried some green gage plums, pears and milk.

Submarines are apt to be about during the late afternoon and early evenings. Guards are on two at a time. Boats are so cleverly camouflaged they look much shorter, like a big yatch. Heard strains of band on boat nearest us.

September 15, 1918—Sunday—Seventh day—Still feel wobbly, but this has really been a wonderful day for me. Services were held in the dining room about 10:00 o'clock. Larkin and I went to portside of deck and said rosary afterwards, returning to starboard side. I spent all day on deck-had tea in lounging. It is served every afternoon at 4:00 p.m. with sandwiches and wafers. Went out on port side of deck and enjoyed myself more than any day so far. Several first class sergeants and nurses were there, having a good time. One of the sergeants gave us a steamer rug—we were very comfortable. They did tricks, crazy stunts and sang. After retreat the privates started singing and we joined in. Sunset was most impressive beautiful pink, old rose and grey. After dinner, Conners, Keoch, and I went to lounging room—a Miss Henri played the piano very well, we enjoyed it. I left for my cabin about 9:10—had my bath about 9:30. You are assigned a certain time for your bath, which is every other day. Jumped into bed after getting my emergency things ready. One is supposed to sleep in pajamas, tights, stockings and have blanket, top-coat, lifesaver and shoes in readiness. I have tried to sleep in tights and stockings but they are slipped off before morning. About 10:00 Larkens walked in and asked me if I didn't need a nurse and in came Kempendorff, all dressed up in regulation grey uniform, only this was short, patent leather belt, hair rolled in a tight knot, roughed profusely with a book and hot water bottle in hands. She put on a very severe professional look, she looked a scream.

September 16, 1918—Monday—Quite chilly and very rocky this morning-Am trying to read Kipling's "Diversity of Creatures". Had lunch, rested awhile. The English captain who eats at our table, said a ship was torpedoed off the Irish coast-154 lives lost, 34 were crew. This is our last night to sleep with clothes off, I hear. I think this Captain was a doctor on ship. We will be in danger zone tomorrow. Will be glad when trip is ended-not afraid, what is the use-never think of it—we are as well protected as it is possible to be under the circumstances. I have heard that if one ship in the convoy is torpedoed the others must not stop to rescue but hurry on out of danger. The battleship and cruiser are left to help the unfortunate. A wonderful rainbow, reflection on the water is beautiful.

Setember 17, 1918—Tuesday—Chilly—ocean bottle green. Sat on deck until 11:15 a.m. Went to lounging room, rested and napped a little before fireplace – felt fine. Had afternoon tea with Betty and Lt.Schultz (don't like him). Capt. Bailey sat down with us. After dinner Conners and I sat in smoking room. Feeling not so good.

September 18, 1918—Wednesday—Morning quite chilly, afternoon windy, misty, hailed some. Evening, foggy and sea roughest and wildest it has been so far. Almost looks as though some of the boats will never get over the waves they are so tossed about. I went to the lounging room danced a little.

September 19, 1918—Wednesday-The boat is rocky—feel miserable—vomited some—felt better. Light lunch, rested and a brisk walk. Read. Everyone is trying to decide what to wear I slept in everything but my dress and shoes, rested good, too. Some of the girls left everything on. Our convoy was met by guards at 10:00 p.m. There apparently had been some anxiety about us.

September 20, 1918—Friday—Woke up happy and wondering at commotion outside—but not for long did I wonder—heard talk of land. I dress quickly, went out on the deck and said "top o' the morning" to Ireland. Later on about 9:30 a.m. viewed the coast of Scotland, the Irish coast vanished about 3:00 p.m. Through field glasses Ireland looked like an awry checkerboard. Scotland coast was still in view. I understand a number of our ships go to Glasgow—rather imagine only a few. Rathlin Island (which I didn't see) is a little dot in the middle of where the Atlantic keeps the Scotch and Irish apart. About here a ship decides which way to go, Glasgow or Liverpool. Quite foggy and misty. I am O.D. (officer of the day) from 4 until 6—had tea first. 5:00 p.m. can't see Scottish coast. Had a glimpse of the isle of Mann (don't seem to remember this), it lies between Ireland and Scotland.

September 21, 1918—Saturday—Really didn't sleep at all last night. Packed what I could, sewed on my collar, cuffs and on blue silk waistband and climbed into bed, shortly after the ship stopped and it felt as though we had been stranded on a sand bar. I don't know what it was, just what it seemed like to me. It started again soon and I was almost asleep when Mrs. Honkenon came in our cabin—said we are to get up at 3:00 a.m. It was after 2:00 then—She said a bugle would blow but I didn't hear it until 4:00 a.m. I was dressed and ready as I couldn't sleep or rest. Went on deck everyone seemed to be there. We had arrived safely in Liverpool. It was lovely—The water, the ships, the beautiful sky with a full moon and the lights in the harbor. Whenever I think of Liverpool, I am sure I shall remember it as it was on our arrival. Had breakfast early, watched the troops leaving. One of the officers, asked for my address and he gave me his with a wish that I might be attached to the 84th division.

We left boat about 8:30 and marched to a waiting room, which is part of a bridge like affair. 18 miles long, built since the war, I've heard. A pier, I guess. Here we identified our luggage, ate lunch, which was given us before we left the boat. Talked to some American boys, walked out a short way from the pier or station, saw a number of dirty little urchins, bold as possible, asking for some American coins and pennies. One of the ladies in the redcross canteen was a former nurse, she has been here 3 years, married a sea captain recently—says America is home and nothing can be compared with it. We got coffee from her. Saw Mrs. Vernon Castle (dancer) who came over on the Migantic white star line with the "C" girls. She was with three English officers in the docks. We left Liverpool about 2:00 o'clock in the quaintest little coaches—All separate from each other. The car or coach held six, on one side were chairs and tables with picturesque scenes of Kallarney and other parts of Ireland—The other half of the coach was velvet cushioned covered seats holding

8—14 in an entire coach. 1st, 2nd, and 3rd class compartments of the express trains are very comfortable but you are facing your fellow travelers. In some coaches there are no corridors but in most a corridor along one side. We were very tired but enjoyed the country, never the less. The buildings are mostly brick, some stone, such a peaceful, quiet contented beauty. The country, all green, it's quaint brick and stone homes are ivy covered, hedges bordering the fields and along the tracks, and always flowers, almost like a park. In Birninghan we had a short stop. Got coffee supposedly, didn't taste like anything pleasant. It was dark by this time and I was tired and nervous, tried to rest but was not very successful. I traveled with lights out. We reached Southampton about 1:30 a.m.

September 22, 1918—Sunday—Southampton—We had to line up and be counted and after much conversing and rearranging, we identified our baggage and 25 of us were sent to "the crown" some were sent to Y.M.C.A. and remainder to another hotel. Brodrick, Larken, and I were put into "16" Wellington. Had a good rest, got into bed about 3:00 a.m. had cider before going to bed—got up at 11:00. Had lunch about 12:00 o'clock, it was tasteless. I was hungry the night before and on an empty stomach, meat didn't go very well. We took a short walk saw an old stone wall or gate built at the time of the Romans and at one time, the only entrance into the city. This is from a guide book. Bargate South Hampton originally, "Barred Gate" once the principal entrance into town. It dates from 1350, though its base is probably far older. The various armorial bearings displayed are those of noble families who have been connected with the town in the past. Southame Tune, given by the Saxons, is richly endowed with relics of past but most famous is Bargate. Am so glad we saw it as we had no time for sightseeing. Saw some German prisoners who had just landed, went back to hotel. We weren't allowed to leave again. Boutillier, Brosch and I had some coffee. English girls we saw all were smoking. American officer was with one in hotel. We left hotel at 3:00 p.m. marched to Southwestern Hotel, were counted and with part of "C" fifty girls, were again marched to the docks and were put on Gloucester Castle, a hospital ship. We were put in a seventy-five bed ward. Brosch, Keach, Broderich, Larkin and I at upper end—We had supper at 6:00 o'clock. Left port at 7:00 o'clock. The largest navy and army hospital along English Channel. Ketels, Kempendorff and I went to dinning room, got some port wine (the steward let me keep a wine glass) and went to bed. I thought it would prevent me from getting sick and it did in this way I went sound asleep and on awakening in the a.m. viewed the coast of Normandy and France. I woke up once in night, 2:00 a.m., think we were nearing French shore then.

Nora in 1918

September 23, 1918—Thursday—Seemed mighty good to be in a French port and know that my ocean voyaging and sea sicknesses are about ended. "La Harve" was our port—we were anchored at the mouth of the Seine River and stayed there until the following morning. We got up rather early, had breakfast at seven—tried to eat but didn't feel very well. We washed all our soiled clothes, manicured our finger nails, washed our hair and rested. At 4 p.m. R.A.M.C. (Royal Army Medical Corps) boys served tea and the best cakes—most of us were in bed—surely tasted good. We pulled up to dock at 11:00p.m.

September 24, 1918—Friday—Got up at 6:45—dressed hurriedly and went out on deck and saw some troops unloading—They were boys who came in our convoy—saw nearly all the officers who came over on our boat "The Melita". We got off our boat "Glowchester Castle" lined up and were sent to two different hotels. I was in group that was sent to Hotel Continental. Had a lovely room all mirrors and an open balcony with French windows. Broderick, Broach, Larkin, Keach and I cleaned up a bit and went sight seeing—and a little shopping. Broderick, Keach and I got tomatoes, grapes, cheese, bread, mustard, apples, salt, and condensed milk. Went back to hotel and had our dinner, very good. We were first served vegetable salad, celery, tomatoes and lettuce with French dressing, 2nd course fish (shad) I think, and 3rd meat course, then grapes. After dinner, at a quarter to twelve we got ready to leave. Ten from our hotel, Keach, Brosch, Mueller, Files, Burns, Conner, and myself, don't remember others and Miss Washburn had charge of us. A Captain Ross was at the depot to look after us—and tend to our baggage and give a few instructions after we were in our carriage—Had a fine trip from Le Harve to Paris. Some officers were on the same train and they came and sat with us until we reached Paris. A Major had charge. There were three Captains and a Lieutenant of the Engineers, doctors and ordinance. They had some rations with us and got off at a station, bought some delicious hard and juicy apples, figs, raisins, nuts and wine—with our bread, jam, beans and canned corned beef we had a good meal. We sang and talked. I asked one poor officer what some sigh in French meant. I should have known better, but I was so impulsive sometimes. I felt like a fool—never again. Mueller had her old Ukelele. The girls in our coach were Day, Buriss, or Bures (I wonder if it wasn't Burns—can't read my writing)—Mueller, Conner, Kaufman, Krogh, Weber, McMullen, Koch, Brodrick, Brosch and I. We reached Paris about 9:30 p.m. all in pitch darkness, a few blue shaded lights in places. Had to carry our suitcases for the first time and besides I had the groceries we had purchased that morning in La Harve. We were lined up again and counted and after some waiting, marched through the depot and were put in trucks, with our suitcases and groceries and oh so glad to get there. We were taken to Continental Hotel and assigned to rooms. Brodrick and I took room 405 (might have been 403) Brosch and Koch 401 next to us. They were dear rooms, plenty of mirrors, twin beds, linen-stitched real linen, old blue velvet hangings and blue panels. Woodwork and walls in white, the furniture Mahogany. We got to bed as soon as possible.

September 25, 1918—Wednesday—We were called about 4:45 a.m. How we hated to leave our nice beds and rooms. We sat around in lobby until all were there and were again placed on trucks and taken to P.L.M. depot.

Landed at quay at Le Havre to Paris, France with its gay colored homes, graceful rolling slopes and fertile fields, its well kept woodland and its trim gay gardens. The quaint high two-wheeled carts with its round roof of heavy linen, dark blue or green and peasant in his bright blouse attract the eye. Sense of poverty in the landscape (trees). The chateaus and manors set back in perfect ancient parks have a heartache about them. They look abandoned and quite. Evidently there is no one to pay for a life of hospitality within their walls. They have a dignity and gentle perfection of form and setting that no other land can boast of in its homes of the same type, something of elegance and tradition of calm simplicity. Great trees, alleys of them, no longer trim to even shape and still give a grand air to the approach. High walls and graceful grilling of wrought iron add the proper note of privacy one loves. Between Havre and Rouen the Chateau has that trait of perfection—that they returned attention.

Rouen, in the ancient tower where Joan of Arch was held prisoner before her execution, a beautiful cathedral.

I suppose P.L.M. means Paris, Lyons, Marville. Then through the fault of officials or Miss. Washburn, who had charge of our suitcases and rations, everything was left behind. Through the kindness of boys on the way, we got bread and jam, certainly enjoyed our groceries. Conner, Mueller, Files, Koch, Brosch, Brodrick, and I were together. Arrived at Meves-Buley at 4 p.m. Met the rest of our unit at Cosne a few stations up. Walked about a quarter of a mile to Base Hospital and were put in ward B1-B2. There were cots for all, sheets, pillows, slips, and three blankets. We made our beds, sheets had been used, so I slept on blanket. We had supper in patients mess—the menu was hash, potatoes, breads and coffee and jam—we were hungry and it tasted awfully good. Took a walk found that unit number 50 was located here. Six of our Camp Lewis girls were in it. Seemed fine to see them. Got to bed about 9:30 and slept. The names of some of the girls: Maron, Inger, Mome, Thompson, Gamble.

September 26, 1918—Thursday—Got up twenty minutes of eight, had breakfast, fussed around ward and went for a walk—Fricke, Bartling, Brosch and I walked to the little village (Mesues—pronounced Mene) brought some grapes, needles and a dictionary—seemed filthy to me. Had dinner and nearly all the girls went on duty. Larkin hid in every available place afraid she might go on duty and we wouldn't. Boutillier, Brosch and I didn't go on. Did go over in evening wanted to do something, give baths etc, but found nothing to do. Unless one is assigned they are not particularly wanted.

September 27, 1918—Friday—We four stayed in bed—nothing to do and some people became much concerned—Brady came in and gave us advice as usual. Conner was sweet, brought toast and coffee and we had some bread and jam, good breakfast. Got up, sewed buttons on my clothes. Lots of excitement later on fifteen girls to be sent out. Six new girls are ill. It is so damp, no pane in windows, everyone has a cold. Surely hope I keep well. Two girls are very sick—Hardy especially—McMullen too, but she has nothing to say. "McMullen" died later—do not know about Hardy.

September 28, 1918—Saturday—Got up at 6:10 went to breakfast half dressed back to bed afterwards to keep warm. Tried to write after lunch, went to commissary after lunch got a box of stick candy and beans, also some men's socks to wear with boots.

Saw Mason—Heard two hundred and fifty boys from 91st division came in. Went to Meves or Mesves. Heard we were leaving for the front, hope so—several different groups. We got packed and ready to leave at 3:30 p.m. Then after the usual waiting found out we weren't leaving until Monday. Betty Brosch and I went over called on patients, found a few from Minnesota came back met some of the girls—Betty went back to Base 50—Mason came over and later Morris and Thompson. Took a bath before going to bed (in a pail) or rather with its half.

September 29, 1918—Sunday—(Dodes Birthday)

Got up 6:20 for breakfast. Put my soiled clothes to soak the night before and while waiting for hot water—walked over to see Mason and on to Headquarters to see if Camp Lewis boys had arrived—no one knew. When we got back Boutillier had taken our hot water, we had to wait until 10:30—finished our washing hung it out, rested, read and dinner. After dinner went down to see about carry-alls, found mine O.K. expect to get it tomorrow. Back to ward met Mason & were going to meet Sergts. Rasmussen, Corp. Barnes & another but went to Buliling and from there to Garrse instead. Nice little village—had the best fried potatoes, steak and omelet, but it was a long way and I was tired when I reached ward.

September 30, 1918—Monday—Didn't get up for breakfast—was washed by eight o'clock hearing everyone talking about being on the 9:30 train and soon left for the station. Some beans, sandwiches and coffee was passed about 1:30 p.m. I was starved. Left about 3:30. Reached Cosne about 5:30. Our baggage was placed in waiting room with an American to look after it and we started looking for something to eat. Had our supper at some officers mess. One of the boys gave me a can opener, which we needed. Left about 7:00, traveled all night.

Tuesday, October 1,1918—Tuesday—Reached _____ about 7:00 a.m. Left there at 10:30 and reached Chatillon Luesese about noon. Some Captain next to us said a truck would be at the station at 1 p.m. to take us to headquarters for dinner. While waiting, some boys (Engineers) asked us to go to one of their kitchens, which we did. Brosch, Conner, Kaufendorf, a little medic and Aheam, a boy from Albert Lea, Minnesota, who knew Ray Shehan. gave us canteens, never had I received anything so welcome—had them filled with water, coffee, enough from them was like a new lease on life. Larkin and Bell were left here sick. Left 4:45 p.m. reached Claremont at 11:00 p.m. Stood in streets about an hour and were then taken to Base Hospital 15. A group of Frenchmen gathered around gave us a good looking over, while we were waiting.

October 2, 1918—Wednesday—9:30 a.m. reached Rinecourt at 10:30 a.m. Were met at the station by one of the boys, a Captian Kenendorf, and Bartling was left to watch luggage and a Miss. Vares to watch 10s. The remainder marched to the hospital.

Mrs. Washburn, Cleary and the Captain leading the way, we are given use of a ward all nice and clean, clean linen and blankets, straw ticks and side curtains of sheets between each bed making it quite private. Dinner was served at 12:45. Stew, very good potatoes, bread and coffee. After dinner we all had the privilege of a shower-it was a great funny sight as it was one large room, cement floor, several showers as it could only be used a certain length of time, we all gathered in there at the same time. After our bath we took a walk into the village, really quite lovely. Enjoyed it so much. stopped at commissary. Back just in time for supper, took a short walk after seating. Got enough hot water to give our faces a good cleaning and wash some handkerchiefs, union suits and stockings and later heated some water for our bottles, warm bed and hardy rest.

Thursday October 3, 1918—Thursday—-Woke and dressed for breakfast at 6:45 oatmeal, pancake, apricots and coffee. Couldn't leave our quarters until finding out about our next move. I remember distinctly of visiting village again and going through a chateau at village which was said to be he home of Napoleon and a beautiful park—sundial—kitchen utensils of copper and in the bedroom a bed of Napoleon

Wooded hills and country surrounding is called the third section of Gaul in time of Ceasar. He is said to have placed a tomb on this hill and there caves and tunnels all the way through. The country is seen for miles around.

October 5, 1918—Friday—Left for Claremont. Had dinner in officers mess (Apparently from my old diary we went back to Charmont instead of leaving for St. Dizier directly from Rinacourt. Reached St. Dizier about 11:00 o'clock a.m. (changed time.) Here the girls were parceled out for the night. Brosch and I were in group that went to Hotel that was filthy place. We were ghastly tired, we placed our coats on the bed, left our clothes on and had a rest, even if not satisfied. Five more of our girls were sent to our American camp and Kemen Dorff said she was given a cot some negro had given up. Some of the boys must have had to get up in order to give nurses their beds. have a feeling I should sit up.

October 6, 1918—Sunday—We got something to eat at a café a sort of dingy old place. Left St. Dizier about 8:10 a.m. Our carriage or portion of it, one entered the door and seats were crosswise, no axle very much by ourselves. Where possibly six could be seated quite comfortably. We were eight packed like sardines all night. Of course we wouldn't want to fuss even to ourselves but truly it was maddening to sit so long. I couldn't cross my knees without upsetting things. Next to us the box car started with the troops jammed in. A number of the officers were drunk, but not all. They were on their way to the front and perhaps this was a chance to forget for awhile. One newly made shave tail was so nice. A man from Annarbor.

October 7, 1918—Monday—traveled all night with no lights had to go very slow. Reached Fleury, a railhead early, in am. and were taken from there by ambulances to evacuation hospital number 11. Situated at the edge of the Argonne Forrest. The villages of Brizeaux not far away. It was around 8:30 when we finally reached base

75

hospital—weary—a tent was erected for us and beds put up—mud, wet, and rain.

October 8, 1918—Tuesday—Woke up about 6:15 rested but it was troubled rest—ambulances continually arriving all night. Miss Connor brought us in our appointment slips. I am to go on night duty on ward K evacuation. There are five in all. Had breakfast and went back to bed. Got up for lunch, cleaned my suit and got my uniform out—wrote a letter or two and covered up to keep warm in bed—of course they are setting in mud. Went on duty at 7:00 p.m. Ward filled up during the night and over bed cots placed in the aisle (all ether cases.) Gassed cases are not given ether. Went to bed immediately going off duty at 7:00 a.m.

October 9, 1918—Wednesday—Enos' birthday, precious darling how I love him, how I miss him (Enos was Nora's younger brother killed by lightning at a very young age). I must not think of it, must be glad for so many things and not complain. So much suffering caused by this war. Sorry about John and Joseph. I must not think or I will go wild. I pray to God that he will spare them. Got in forty eight cases and I was so tired. My back hurts so. The cots are low and I so much want to help. Tried to wash faces and hands of as many as I could. They will all be gone and new cases will be arriving soon during the night. It is so pathetic and funny too. One will curse the dirty Hun and another praying for the Lord to give him strength to get back to the firing lines. Another crying and calling mama, someone else wondering if his comrade got away, others laughing, hysterically wondering if mama will be glad when he returns. Still another will swear "I'll never leave home if I ever get there."

Hot doughnuts rare treat—I guess, airplane raid reported early in the sky.

October 10, 1918—Sunday—Could hear the guns bombing away but don't believe there was any barrage. Sky was not lit up. This is a thirty day drive, hope the war will end before that time is up. So many boys are being sacrificed. Twenty one ether cases tonight. I laughed until I nearly cried—one poor fellow said" O Missus, Missus, my dear "Ver" and another coming out of ether, had to be held in bed, he wanted to get the German that killed his pal. Had a regular croup when I awoke up today. Do wish I was over this nasty cold.

October 11, 1918—Monday—Washed some. Met a Schoemscock from Rochester, Minn. Came in with a leg wound. Had a good sleep in morning until 10:00 then could not rest after. Girl next to me got a letter from home. I cried a little, got up at 4:30—went to supper at 5:15. Miss Washburn, my chief, said I was to go into ward M. officers. Later ironed clothes.

October 13,1918—Tuesday—Fifteen girls left for elsewhere in the night. All were on O ward. Miss Brosch is to be on ward M. with me. I am in charge, everything fine after first day cleaned things generally. Found some cooties.

October 14, 1918—Wednesday—Lt. Scroggin died. Rains all the time shoes are a sight feet never dry. Went over to Kemups after duty from there to Lugerie got trousers to match jacket, french red cross corduroy also a pair of pajamas.

October 15, 1918—Thursday—Bathed and went to bed. Breakfast now changed from 7:00 to 8:30 a.m. I thought the hospital was moving in the night. There was so much noise. Did find out later that an army ambulance tipped outside our quarters. Captain Jeffers, a patient said I must have a guilty conscious. Burm went on duty tonight.

October 16, 1918—Friday—Patients, Captain Jeffers, Lt. Plearants and Lt. Hallquist left today. Lts. Patton, Stuart, Amotti were better. Lt Jacoby very ill-double puenionia, bad back wound, walked through mud and rain after being injured. Betty and I took wash down to laundry. Today took a bath (pail) after returning. Got underwear and socks from quartermaster.

October 17,1918—Thursday—Went down to portable laundry and got clothes we had left. Boys are fine this p.m. After dinner Miss Washburn came on ward and asked me to go to Bar-Le-Duc to buy rubber overshoes, anything to keep our feet dry. One of the nurses from A team asked to go with me. Three officers took us, a Major with the English Army and two Lieutenants. Had a time finding something to eat. Got home late, was almost dead.

October 18, 1918—Friday—Laundry (repeat) Went to movie in French camp—laughed. Conner was there she had been transferred to pneumonia and influenza camp near by. Tired.

October 19, 1918—Saturday—My watch was wrong and as was Betty's so I went over to ward and made Betty go to breakfast. We finished boiling our clothes, cleaned our shoes etc. Betty took from one to three and I took one to five. Was in my room when I heard Boutillier she had been in 58 sick. Glad to get back to their group. She told us of Anna McMullens death. I was shocked she was truly a lovely girl. Betty and I ironed our uniforms and capes.

October 20,1918—Sunday—Lt. Brindjove asked me to go for a walk. I wouldn't but did go to dinner this evening with him, Took Betty to a French officers men's Remount station. We really had a wonderful time Two Captains made us feel very much at home

Several coffees later and a little wine, the newly made Captain played the piano for us. A selection from the Pink Lady, National French songs, we hummed as he sang the Marseille. Left about ten o'clock. Could almost think I was not to far from home.

October 21,1918—Monday—Lt. Jacoby worse, moved screen in, stimulants and oxygen. Went to bed early.

October 22, 1918—Tuesday—Lt. Jacoby died—cleaned kitchen.

October 23, 1918—Wednesday—Captain Funach, Betty, Lt. Brindjove and I caught rides to Verdun. On the way stopped at French aviation field, Brindjove speaks French. He was born in Jersey—it was convenient—On the way back we took a shortcut and walked all together 18 miles, we were so thirsty. On reaching some little village Lt. Brindjove got some wine Vin Rouge or Vin Blanc-anyhow it was like taking vinegar and my mouth and lips were parched and caked. Capt. Funach let us rest short minute. Once we sat down close almost on an ammunition dump and the Jerry Liberty planes were roaring over head the red and green lights-like stars shooting down and the putt, putt of guns—the search lights playing I looked and saw but didn't care much what was happening to me. As we neared Brizeaux we had our last rest, but I wanted to stay right there. I laid down against a bank and used my gas mask for s pillow. No bed could ever feel better. Capt. Funach soon started us on our way again and I felt as though I couldn't manage another foot. We had talked about getting something to eat after leaving Verdun. It was impossible for me to eat, although I did go to kitchen and set down while rest ate. Capt. Bailey was there and a few others.

October 24 1918—Thursday—Everyone is kidding us about our long walk. Capt. Furach stopped in to say hello. Lt. Krog, Dunn, Kemp and Burns teased us frightfully. Dunn and Brindjove asked us to a chicken dinner, said yes but tried to back out. Dunn explained that Capt. Hunter was giving it and would be offended of course. We went and sort of enjoyed. I was so stiff and I felt I was going to faint. Too exhausted to sleep.

October 25, 1918—Friday—Felt half and half this morning and I am so stiff, so stiff. Straightened up our room. Betty and I did our little washing. Vomited-felt some better. Late in p.m. had hot milk, toast and jam. I came to my room with hot water bottle and two candles (to use as light). Betty came over early-Miss Washburn came in for a few minutes. Felt better, worked a few minutes. Washed my hair sitting in bed—dandy wash.

October 26, 1918—Saturday—Got up and went on duty, felt sick shortly after-Miss Washburn happened by and took me to her room. She is good and her room is very cozy and nice. She tucked me in and I stayed there until noon, and then I went to my own room and to bed. Betty brought me some canned tomatoes and salt, they tasted good. Miss Washburn went through barracks about 10 o'clock calling pay role to be signed. Went over for supper. Betty did my hair bow—ironed.

October 27, 1918—Sunday—Beautiful day—intended going to mass but poor Capt. Young had his hand amputated this a.m. He is a wonderful fellow, so good, never complains and he must suffer frightfully. He lost so much blood, he is having a hard time, looks so white and thin. Furach, Dunne and Shields were in also Major Roach and Brindjove. Brindjove said he had a piece of stained glass from the Cathedral window for me. I think he got it from St Margaret's
Lee Nioms from the kitchen fried a steak and potatoes for Betty and I and Lt. Neubold. A Lt. Quinn happened in looking for an officer and we gave him and his chauffer dinner and also divide with Lunderman. Surely was awfully good. Lt. Quinn said he would come back this way and take us for a ride. Lt. Quinn returned later, it was some what crowded in the Dodge Roadster with a chauffer, Lt. Quinn and Betty and I. Got in bed about 10:00 p.m.

October 28, 1918—Monday—Worked in a.m. and p.m.! Betty and I with Sergeant Lambert walked up on top of a big hill to Belem. Went through an old grave yard. One tombstone was 135 years old. There may have been older. The view was wonderful. Went to bed early.

October 29, 1918—Tuesday—Betty and I sewed on our blankets and bathrobes. She came back to the ward. Several officers were in. In the evening just as I was going off duty Lt. Quinn and a friend of his, Murray, came. Lt. Dunn walked while they were there. We all went to Les-Islets. We walked around, had cocoa bread and jam and brought some German helmets.

October 30, 1918—Wednesday—Miss Washburn told Betty and I at breakfast that we could have the day off. After coming back from breakfast two boys said they were going to St. Menebould so we hurriedly put on our suits and went with them. Did some shopping and visited a church. Met some boys from Florent. We went in the truck to their camp. They told us one of the Roosevelts was stationed here. From there around to Les Islets with Capt. Johnson. Met a Lt. Brown. Decided to come back home and met Capt. Steyers-walked part of the way. Lunch in mess.

October 31, 1918—Thursday—Danced at Raton in laundry. Dunn and a bunch went with us, boys were stationed at Argonne on the way to the front. I came home. Got lunch in our kitchen.

November 1, 1918—Friday—Boutillier and I went to Afremont with an ambulance driver—saw the front lines. A French plane down in a field to our right, and saw several newly made graves, with a stick placed at the head of each with their identification tags nailed on. In Xheville was stone standing upright.

November 2, 1918—Saturday—Ward M to Ward 2. Worked all day.

November 3, 1918—Sunday—Could not manage church.

November 4, 1918—Monday—Ward 2, general cleaning

November 6, 1918—Wednesday—Lt. Dussue cane over to room, Keiafeudorff, Bondell were in. Broach made fudge.

November 8, 1918—Friday—Meeting at Verdun of war staff to discuss armistice, our news grows.

November 11, 1918—Monday—To make up their minds, firing ceased at 4p.m. Started again.

French artillery and American Calvary passing by to and from the front, all the poor wounded boys. I hear their stories, see them and know that half isn't told, and when I go on duty and whether it is a quite rain on a lovely moon to see, by 11:o'clock, the same sky is lit up with the lights of warfare and the rumble of guns and you wonder why over and over. Eighteen airplanes went by late, look s like many more traveling the sky in the evening.

Order of Medical and Surgical Detachment(Regimental Aid Station) First, ambulance, then field hospital, evacuation, and finally base. Sometimes the field hospital was done away with particularly where evacuation was near to front. Heard since, they were done away with almost all together.

Nov. 15, 1918—Friday—Night duty

Nov. 16, 1918—Saturday—Night—Ward M. Captain Young, I think he is most patient fellow, afraid he will not get well.

Nov. 17, 1918—Sunday—Up for dinner. Armistice seems to good to be true—hardly seems a realization. Now the after affects of this horrible war. So thankful as it is.

Nov. 18, 1918—Monday—Dance at Raton

Nov. 19, 1918—Tuesday—Sent over to ward F, no very sick patients. Then sewed on A's (our insignia) all p.m. Dunn and Brindjove were over. Sewed an A on Capt. Fuach's coat. Was awfully worried when I reached my quarters after duty and was partly undressed when Bartlett came in and asked me to go out with an officer, Lt. Stong. A friend of the officer she was going with, Lt.

Jefferson. They were both connected with Brizaux. Did not want to go, but she insisted I go and finally made me decide by saying she had helped me out before. Lt. Stong was tall, 6 foot 3" and rather quiet, and felt like he was kind of bored. We walked over to Raton and back. He asked me to come down to Brizaux the following evening, Battling was to be there and Edgar to pair off with Woodbury. Consented to go, Brizaux was an over flow hospital (or was to be) and Lt. Stong was in charge and it was organized under him. Jefferson, Woodbury, and Deurue were with him. Later it was found that this American army was moving so fast and the over flow would not be needed but after the Armistice, it still remained—One of the young orderlies, Fleetwood, Broach and I had with us when we just went on Ward M, was sent to Brizaux when it was open. We stopped in to see him on our way to church one Sunday morning and I remember seeing Lt. Stong there. Saw his name several times, thought it I must be Strong. Fleetwood was hardly more than 16, think Broach and I had a motherly interest in him. Called him Cupid.

Lt. Elliott Stong

Nov. 20, 1918—Wednesday—Sewed on more A's for Jimmie, George, Vlaich and Moe—such nice boys. Went down to Brizeaux this evening Lt. Stong and I went over to his room and stayed a short time. Large room, Lt. Dunn rooms with him, rather barren, beds and a few chairs & table but the big fireplace, which is kept going when they are in room makes it very cheery. Went over to Jefferson's & Woodbury's room—Edgar—Bartling were there. They had Champagne and doughnuts—my first drink of champagne and it made me feel rather queer so Lt. Stong and I left and took a walk. I am surprised Edgar would touch it—she seems to straight laced and sedate. Stopped in Lt. Stong's room a few minutes. Home by 10:30. Like him.

Nov 21, 1918—Thursday—I think the boys expected to have a feast last night but failed to get their steak etc. so asked us down for to-night. Here I am to go on night duty in Ward M. Burris in G. So I gave a note to Jimmie to give to Lt. Stong as he was coming up between 1 and 3 on my hours, but as we had the day off we wanted to go someplace. We started out in an ambulance for Bar-Be-Due only got as far as Frully. There is a big dump here. The largest thing of its kind, all sorts of supplies. We met a Lt. Davis and he gave us a leather jerkin—introduced us to Major Cook, a regular army man, who is in charge. Rough and unkempt but he loaded us down with candy and gave us each a scarf and insisted on us staying for dinner. There mess was called Hotel Scruinole—I believe after a hotel in Jacksonville Florida. They had a flag-raising, the pole had just been made ready the day before. Betty and I and several high up officers stood around the pole—we were thrilled. 900 German prisoners were lined up across the road to watch proceedings. We went up to Varennes after, saw their tanks.

Nov. 22, 1918—Friday—Capt. Reynolds O.D., stayed on Ward 17. Crazy old married man I wonder if he thinks that I am feeble-minded. Slept good all day. Lt. Stong and Jefferson were up last night. He came up this evening. I talked to him a short time-Walked down to laundry and back. He asked to call tomorrow evening-went out for a little walk. Told him abut Reynolds and he suggested I speak to Miss Washburn.

Nov. 23, 1918—Saturday—Told Miss Washburn, she put me on ward H and moved Edgar on ward M. I was so mad at him I could have cried he followed me around. Spent from 6:00 to 7:30 with Lt. Stong

Nov. 24, 1918—Sunday—Went to church—walked this evening.

Nov.25,26,27—Walked each evening with Lt. Stong.

Nov. 28, 1918—Thanksgiving—Have so much to be thankful for-my brothers are all well or safe. Out of this dreadful war and can go home without the terrible memory of the battlefield. Brasch and I stayed in bed all day, to lazy to get up even for a good dinner. After supper had a phone call from Major Cook. He was over in the morning but I asked Boots to tell him I was asleep. He told me over the phone that Major Porter had left Fluery and would probably soon be here for us. I tried to find someone to go in my place but couldn't. The girls wanted us to go. Boutiller, Bartling, Brosch and I had a perfectly gorgeous dinner, danced with Major, Lt. Colonel etc. We were showered with candy. Major Cook acted a fool though. Never again. Lt. Stong came over for a few minutes after I got home.

November 29, 1918—Friday—Went for a walk with Lt. Stong after supper. Lt. Brindjove came overt to Ward for a visit and while he was there Major Cook and Lt. Krog came in. Major Cook absolutely is the most rudest. He tries to make one think they are compelled to do as he bids. He went so far as to give Colonel Diwal my name. Boots, Bartling and Burch asking him to see that we were sent in the group to a dance at Fluery tomorrow night. He also went to Miss Washburn. I am ashamed.

Nov. 30, 1918—Saturday—Danced at Fluery. Farwell for some thirty officers who are leaving. Several of the girls went over. Major Cook came over and cursed because Boots, Brosch and I would not go. I am mighty glad I had enough sense to remain at home. Only man I have met since being in the Army that I have a fear of. Lt. Stong and I went for a walk. Met a truck going over with a group of girls. Told him I would answer a question he asked soon perhaps the following night. I like him so well.

December 1,1918—Sunday—Church. Lt. Stong and Jefferson up this evening. Very few in ward, no sick patients. Left ward alone with Bartling and Jefferson with Miss Washburn permission until 10:30 p.m. It was raining, went to Lt. Stong's room. It was so pleasant in his room-nice fire. I told him the answer to his question, how much I cared for him. I hardly think he needed an answer for surely I have shown him so very much I liked him. I didn't want to. Now I shall have to write to Charlie, Johnny, Jim and Harry Klinger. Funny things happen. I really didn't want to marry any of them and I do Elliott, he is so fine. Bartling and Jeffererson had some champagne. No more for me.

December 2-3, 1918—Passavant Road-lonely nights, wonder what is planned for this hospital. Doesn't seem we will be her much longer.

December 4-5, 1918—Last of nights for awhile, Dunn and Brindjove are peeved

December 6, 1918—Friday—To Brizeaux with Elliott.

December 7, 1918—Saturday—Met him again this evening at Officers' dance in ward M good time. Vememan looked thru widow-told me he got his enjoyment watching Elliott and I. "He is big and you are little." He was an orderly when Brosch and I were on ward M.

December 8, 1918—Sunday—Edgar, Bartling, Burns, Borsch and I went to church. We laughed at Burns because she refused the bread, passed in little baskets, they are small cubes of bread, and is passed as a form of courtesy, a welcome to strangers (breaking of bread)—customary in France. Passed during offertory of mass. Elliott came in the evening.

December 9, 1918—Monday—Slept, read a letter, will see Elliott this evening.

December 10, 1918—Tuesday—On the way back from dinner saw a little old Ford standing at entrance to hospital grounds, stopped to look at it, two boys came along and we all went for a ride with them, Brosch, Bartling, Edgar and I. They were from German prison camp outside Triacourt. We stooped there and I drove an old horse from their camp to the village. Met Capt. McGovern who is in charge. We went through village church with him, and when we got back Capt. McGovern and I went out shooting (practicing) I think I hit the mark once. Later he and I went horse back riding. The girls had left when we returned. So Capt. McGovern got his driver and he brought me back to hospital. Met Elliott about 6:45. Capt. McGovern had lovely quarters in a French home in village-the garden back of home is lovely even now and must be beautiful in Spring and Summer.

December 11,1918—Wednesday—Got up in time to go to dinner with Capt. McGovern at Triacourt-went horse back riding immediately after. Passed thru some wonderful pretty woods. I was on Capt. McGovern's horse, he was so spirited, and galloped so fast. Capt McGovern was frightened and rode up along side and tried to catch bridle. My horse jumped a ditch and broke a fence. I was quite thrilled for I thought I could hang on. Boutller and Edgar went home with Bartling driving. Capt. McGovern and I went to Fleury. Bartling stayed and I went on to Souilly, nearly stalled there. Went back by Fleury for Barlting. Arrived home in time to meet Elliott. Enlisted men dance on ward M.

December 12, 1918—Thursday—Elliott and I in Edgar's room next to ours. Played poker and rummy. Brownie and Brosch in our room.

December 13, 1918—Friday—Elliott moved from Brizeaux to hospital today and closed the hospital down there. His quarters are on ward M. Bartling, Boutilline, Burns, Brooks and I started out for our walk, Burns and Edgar ahead. Boots and I came back for money. Broach and Bartling who started later caught up with us on our return. We met Elliott on the road with Sgt. Denver and got in the truck with them and rode to Brizeaux from there to Passavant and Triacount and back. Then Boots and I chased all over for kindling, finally decided to go to Les Isellets for wood and supplies. We were late getting home and Elliott had called and was angry. I was peeved and didn't like it, later I found out that the girls told Boots to keep me out. They didn't like Elliott taking up so much of my time. Edgar, Bartling, Burns and Boots played cards in Edgar's room. Elliott's and I in my room for a while.

December 14, 1918—Saturday—got up rather late. Elliott asked me to go to Souilly with him right after dinner. Swely his driver was with us. Went all around the country as well. We got lost until we reached Reviguy and knew where we were. Swely enjoyed it but looked a sight the old four track had no windshield.

Officers dance fairly good time we came home about 10:30. We stayed in our room until the dance was over.

December 15, 1918—Sunday—Brownie, Brooks Burns and I went to church. Burns walked back with Capt.Timinl. I was with Capt. Shields. Elliott and I spent the evening together. Sgt. Velts and Burns in Edgar's room.

December 16, 1918—Monday—Enlisted man dance in ward H. Broach expected Ralphie over but he couldn't come. Elliott and I walked to Triacourt and back. It started to rain as we came in.

We talked about religion. I hardly knew what to do. I don't want any trouble or disagreeableness afterwards I'd much rather never see Elliott again and I care as much as anybody can. Why can't things be different. He doesn't see any cause to worry but to a Catholic their faith stands above everything.

December 17, 1918—Tuesday—I fussed around my room after getting up at noon. There was a little excitement created by hearing one of the officers say he had the dope as to our next move, that orders were received that we were to be sent to a base at Le Mans. Elliott and I spent time in trunk room. He thinks I am uncertain and haven't been sure but I promised really truly that I would marry him. I told him I had never felt so content and gloriously happy. I want to be worthy of a good home. I am so afraid of being a disappointment. I guess I have an inferiority complex.

Burns was with a group that went over to St. Menebould they visited German dugouts made of concrete. She got a dandy mirror; we all got piece.

December 18, 1918—Wednesday—It's rainy and cold. I told Elliott my age I'm a few years older than he is.

December 19, 1918—After dinner Elliott and I went for a walk it snowed a short time, great big flakes. Then the sun came out after and it was lovely. I hated to go inside after our walk. I went to Briziaux and back wanted to find some gum. Elliott came over in the evening we walked about halfway between Briziaux and Tricourt it was cloudy when we left but was perfectly clear and wonderful before we reached home. We spent remainder of the evening in trunk room until 11:30 We had a blanket to sit on and used old blankets bathrobe. Hope we leave here, it is so cold in our quarters and no place to go. Trunk room is our sitting room it's a dusty old place.

December 20, 1918—I got up for dinner, cleaned and fussed around the room, and wrote a letter. Elliott called about 4p.m.

we went for a short walk and did some practice shooting. Elliott gave me an Italian automatic for my very own. We got back just in time for supper. After supper we cleaned our revolvers. Danced at Fraidos. Brooks, Edgar, Remendorff and I stayed home. Edgar was in Miss Washburn room-Bausch went down later and then they had lunch. Kennendorff to bed early. Elliott and I each drew plans for a home and then one together-talked about a home, and I want to build a real one for him.

Dec.21, 1918—Saturday—Got up at 10:20 a.m. Had a wonderful afternoon. Elliott predicted rain, the sky looked threatening—it didn't. We had our revolvers. It really is a fine feeling not to be afraid of handling one, and I do want to learn how to be a good shot., Elliott is. We walked nearly to Futean. Left at one got back at five. I do care for him so very much, enjoy every minute with him. He came over at 6:45 we cleaned revolvers. Enlisted men's dance—Brosch and Brownie stayed in Burns room-we in mine. Made toast and had tea. Told Elliott I wore a hair piece. He went home about eleven. Edgar, Bartling came in after dance.

Dec.22, 1918—Sunday—Woke up at twenty minutes to eight. Dressed and went to breakfast(bacon and eggs)11a.m. changed clothes and put on suit. Elliott came over at 9 a.m. We started out—Barthing—Freike caught up with us on the other side of Brizeaux and stopped in church. Met Lt. Davis. Back in time for dinner. Trunk room in evening. Elliott wants to send to Tiffany Paris for my ring—think we had better wait.

December 23, 1918—Monday—Aviators at Rembercourt asked us to dinner. I didn't intend to go but they teased the girls so that I decided I would. There was an officers dance and of course I expected to meet Elliott. I skipped over to his quarters to tell him. He was out, so I left word that we would be back for dance. Miss Washburn our chief was going with us. Quite a long way to go-had a perfectly delightful dinner. Wonder where they got everything. drinks with it but I didn't take any. I had a fine fellow for a partner

Lt. Mc Duffee. He didn't drink either-he was from Minneapolis. Washburn, Bortillier, Brosch, Kennendorf, Bartling, Edgar and I went. We were late in getting home and Elliott was furious and so I immediately got on my high horse so to speak. Then he was sorry—Lt. Mc Duffee and the others came to our quarters and tried to get me to go over to dance. I insisted on going, and Elliott and I got as far as the door of ward and then he hated so going in so late and everything that I felt sorry and we went for a walk instead. I was not going to have Elliott "the joke," but I was horrid myself to him. Really our first quarrel. I felt miserable because I was so ugly. He is precious.

December 24,1918—Tuesday—Christmas Eve. Elliott came over at noon, we went for a walk. I think we understand and are sorry to have hurt each other. I wish I were not so sensitive and so stubborn. We had our room tonight. Borsch thought it was her night. Went to midnight mass at Brizeaux—Elliott went with me. Earlier we went for a short walk before mass. It was cold in church—the roof leaked, it had been bombed.

Funny two Frenchman behind us were slightly tipsy, they whispered duing mass and when the basket of bread cubes were passed around a women and a boy in front of us took a fistful each.

Elliott wrote this in my diary after our little quarrel: Oh the comfort, the inexpressible comfort of feeling safe with a person. Having neither to weigh thoughts nor measure words. But pouring all right out just as they are chaff and grain together certain that a faithful hand will take them and sift them. Keep what is worth keeping and with the breath of comfort blow the rest away.

Dec. 24, 1918

N.E.D.

E.S.S.

December 25, 1918—Christmas Day—Got up quite early, went over to Ward H to help Conner, Edgar, and Campbell decorate the Christmas tree. We had a very good dinner at 2:00 p.m.

Evacuation Hospital No. 11

Brizeaux-Forestierre, France

December 25, 1918

Officers Mess Menu for Christmas Dinner

Vegetable soup, roast pork with applesauce, creamed peas, mashed potatoes, stringless beans, marmalade, apples, chocolate fudge, nuts, plum sauce, doughnuts, apple pie, and bread with butter.

Went for a walk with Elliott about 3:30 p.m., back at 5. Went over to supper together, came over to my room at 6:30 p.m. Kemp is sick. I wanted to visit Fluery—did not go. Bausch, Boutillier, Bartling, Burns, Edgar went over. They were late for enlisted men's dance and program. Program was enjoyable. Part of script below. I believe Campbell and Conner (tiny) took the part of bride and groom. Campbell a big tall girl, Conner very small, hardly five feet, Mrs. Washburn the minister.

"Army Romance"

Friends, we are gathered together on a very solemn occasion to cement two hearts that beat as one. The couple before me should think seriously before answering the following questions.

Do you Corn-Willie, take Hardy Tack to be your rock or resistance at all times, no matter what be the conditions of your teeth. (I do)

Do you promise to get up and make the fires, get breakfast, take care of the children and do any other little task your wife may require? (I do)

Do you Hardy Tack promise to take Corn Willie in any way, shape, or manner through thick of thin, hot or cold, for breakfast, dinner and supper, even through burned to a crisp? (I do)

I now pronounce you what is presently called a square meal in the army, bless our children.

December 26, 1918—Thursday—Elliott and I took a long walk, do a little shooting each day. Elliott put a ten centines piece up against a tree, I couldn't hit it of course. He did. Trunk room, don't mind very much I was so tired and Elliott had a headache. Went to bed early—10:00 p.m. Guess our trip to Grand Prix made us all weary. This was a hard fought American point. The forest looked like a fire had swept through and the country in desolation itself. There are a few buildings left in Grand Prix, which is unusual. We came upon several graves of our soldiers in the town. We visited a German cemetery, looks as if they intended it for a permanent one. The square plot fenced in with heavy iron railings and regular tombstones. These dugouts of concrete look compatible. They, the German, built this part of cemetery sometime.

Washburn, Sounumberg, Bortillier, Bartling, Edgar, Finke, Capt. Fuach, Elliott, and Maj. Warnigam all went along.

December 27, 1918—Friday—Got up around 9:30, cleaned my shoes and washed. Elliott went to Les Islettes, this a.m., got some ammunition and went out after 1 p.m. Went into woods, walked up a steep hill and came back by the road—got my feet wet so had to come home.

Elliott left around ten. I love him so much but I am almost afraid and think sometimes it would be better to give him up, then to marry a non-catholic. He can't understand my viewpoint but then only a Catholic would. He has never been baptized, but always attended some church. Kennendorff left, I think for Southern France (is quite sick). Conner moved in her room.

December 28, 1918—Saturday—Breakfast, Elliott and I walked up Passavant road, spent a short time in room.

December 29, 1918—Sunday—I got up in time for breakfast, Brosch got up later and we went to church at Brizeaux. Coming home we saw a little French boy use a tree for his "toilley"—he didn't seem to mind. We got to giggling and then were frightened wondering who was behind us. Prity, Greenmen, Chapples, and Shank were near. Glad we weren't with any men. I had the giggles all day. Elliott, I know wondered what was the matter with me. We walked up Passavant road and over on north side of the woods. Two fellows on horseback were having a heated argument. We were in our room in evening. Finished furnishing our rooms—in our homes to be, my lover and I. Conner and Favinger went to service in Ward H. One of the enlisted men is giving the sermon.

December 30, 1918-Monday—Danced at Triacourt, Conner made some awful good fudge. Captain Fox helped her. Elliott and I talked of many things. I adore him.

December 31, 1918—Tuesday—Minstrel show—we didn't go. On road to Les Islettes, back from road is quite a large home. I was shooting a mark on a tree. Bullet ricocheted over a steep bank and I was frightened, will teach me to be much more careful.

New Years Eve—Aviators came over in big truck with piano, moved into hospital grounds playing and singing. Light snow.

January 1, 1919—Wednesday—

New Year's Day menu.

Roast pork, mashed potatoes with brown gravy, scalloped corn, creamed string beans, olives, celery, dates, grapes, figs, apple pie, cheese, doughnuts, cherry sauce, bread & butter, and coffee.

Oville H. Sowl—Mess Sargent & Lieut. William L. Favinger—Mess Officer

January 2, 1919—Thursday—Danced at Souilly Elliott and I and Conner.

January 3, 1919—Friday—Up for breakfast, packed, went for a walk. Expected to go to Beaulean.

January 4, 1919—Saturday—Left our home in the Argonne forest today, and many sad and many pleasant memories will forever leave it in my mind undeniably written there. Elliott had charge of the baggage he came over in one of the trucks. Sore throat. Saw just a little of him (I expect we were taken over in ambulances.)

January 5,1919—Sunday—On our way—we have fairly good accommodations. Eliott and Capt. Furach come in occasionally to sit with us. Seems wonderfully good to have Elliott for a little while. The officers have second class miserable old board seats.

January 6, 1919—Monday—Edgar was left accidentally in town—we all got out there to walk about a bit and get something to eat. Elliott came to carriage door as we were leaving—said we were going to Camp Hospital #52 at Le Maus and the officers and men to classification camp. I about cried I shall feel lost without Elliott around. He means so much to me—and he is so worried too. Le Maus—we are in Annex 1. Conner, Woodburn, Burns, and I were in same ambulance. I could barely keep the tears back. Met some men from Minnesota at the station—wanted night and darkness to come to be by myself.

Le Maus a quite little cathedral city of central Brittany became over night one of the principal junctions and troop concentration points in the Universe and the Le Maus office of the L.C.A. (Department and Division of Criminal Investigation) developed into a crime-detecting center of metropolitan proportions. Karl W Detzer was Captain in charge of the Le Maus office during the great homeward bound movement of American troops in 1919. I have read series of his stories, thrilling and interesting because they are true. Poutlieu, a suburb of Le Maus, is mentioned frequently. There was the famous forwarding camp.—brick barracks, the River Hires not far away, and the famous gothic cathedrals. St. Julian was a center of interest for all Americans. From Tours to Le Maus, the road was called the Highway of Crosses.

January 7, 1919—Tuesday—Burns and I said we would not leave this place until we either heard from or saw Elliott & Capt. Furach. Really didn't expect them in the morning, but they came—oh—I wanted to hug him there before everyone—I was so happy. Came back in p.m. with mail and again in the evening.

January 8, 1919—Wednesday—Got up at 7 o'clock rushed to breakfast—Conner, Edgar, Hoke, Burns, Bartling, and I went down town. Conner and Edgar got some beautiful linens. I bought two boudoir pillow tops and some handkerchiefs. While gazing at everything in sight, window shopping etc—my sweet heart called me, he with Major Wourgem and an interpreter were looking for a diamond ring—the major knows quite a bit about diamonds, why Elliott took him. After awhile I went in and had my finger measured.

Went up to hotel where officers stay—Elliott went over to A.P.O. called for Ford it wasn't there so we walked out to hospital after lunch. We met Broach, Brownie—Edgar, Hoke & Schultz going out. We went on up to dormitory—Elliott stayed until 2:30 p.m. Had to be back as they were unloading. Back in evening and we went for a walk—while gone Capt. Wymans had called to see me. He was with the Red Cross, knew him at Camp Lewis. Told Elliott who he was, is stationed at Red Cross here in Le Maus—down near Norte Dame church. Miss. Washburn didn't like his looks, she said. I only knew him well enough to speak to him.

My brothers, John & Joseph are now members of the prisoners of war

Jan. 9, 1919—Thursday—Out of bed at 6:30 a.m. After breakfast Edgar fitted the bottom of my Ulster and Broach and I

97

left for the (Le Maus down town about 9:00.) Bought perfume, lace, corset, and stockings. Got a few dates and cookies—reached home shortly after 12, had dinner. Elliott came at 1. We walked over to a little village, St. Pavage, a beautiful road. Up to dormitory after visiting hospital. Elliott left at 5 came back in the evening. A few times we sat in dining room.

Jan. 10, 1919—Friday—Boutillier, Broach, Boots, Edgar, and I went down town. Edgar and Boots got a shampoo. Betty and I a manicure. I bought four pairs of gloves—they are lovely. We had lunch late. Elliott came about 2 o'clock we went out on the south road. In the evening I was cross with Elliott. Think I am getting pretty homesick. Wish I could see John and Joseph. Haven't felt so miserable in ages. I was sorry, Elliott is so good and he wouldn't hurt me for anything. Cried a little, took a bath, felt better. Tomorrow I get my ring. It seems so final and while I am sure and know how sincerely and surely I love my precious lover boy—I think he not being a Catholic frightens me, as to future troubles it might come up and of course when I thought of a husband I thought a Catholic one. Elliott is far better than I am, even if he does not belong to a church. Not because I love him particularly, but he is the most perfect man for I never thought a man would be better than I—he is.

Jan. 11, 1919—Saturday—Washed, finished my coat, shined my shoes. Elliott came out at 1, sat down awhile. Elliott couldn't get ring this a.m. We went down town went through the St. Julian's Cathedral, famous gothic cathedral, then down to the R.E.H.Q. on our way back stopped at Notre Dame, a beautiful little church—some shrine in basement—went back up town got our ring. Had something to eat and evening walked out on the East road—a beautiful night. The white road glistening—we seem to have it all. We stopped by a gate and there my precious put it on my finger. So happy, my wonderful big boy, I love him.

Jan 12, 1919—Sunday—Was last one up, Conner saw my ring when I came in last night. Do not feel very good. Cold and usual thing. Went to Norte Dame to church. Elliott came out about 1:30 p.m. On south road, sat down on ladder to rest. Mrs. Washburn in when we returned—she told all, my ring was wonderful. All the girls raved over it and teased me. Fuach, Burns, Elliott and I went to minstrel.

Jan 13, 1919—Monday—Hoke, Butler, Boots, and I went down town. Took my Ulster and dress to be pressed and cleaned. Bought a rain hat. Grim and Stauffer are with us awhile. Elliott out in the p.m. went for a walk—home early. Elliott got a ride back to town in the Col.'s car. Danced at 52 in evening. Met some nurses and friends of Elliott—they are from Iowa City, Iowa. Capt. Sursch walked out with Burns so Elliott had company home. I was tired.

Jan 14, 1919—Tuesday—Boots and I, after rising, and just before dinner took our collars to a lady near Annex to do up. Elliott and I went out for a walk in the evening. Talked to Conners awhile. Wrote to Charlie, told him as I promised I would, that I knew Elliott was the man I wanted to marry. Charlie proposed to me when I was in my teens and has kept it up ever since. Certainly I have told him that I didn't want to marry him. He is fine and I like him, but he always felt that as long as I wasn't married I might change my mind. He knew I might marry him. I have written to him and Johnny Johnson. Their pride may be hurt and maybe they will feel a trifle hurt but really they are lucky—I'm such a queer person at times—Anyhow my skinny loves me and I don't care about nothing else. Took my diary.

Nora and Elliott on one of their many walks on a cold winter's day

Jan 15, 1919—Wednesday—Broach and I went to the hospital to see the girls who are sick. Elliott came up about 1:30—started out for walk but came back—stayed awhile in hall. Called on Weber—Elliott's driver. Elliott not feeling well, went to Majors room. He came back in evening—walked awhile rained quite hard, came back, got key to dinning room—Doughnuts—Brought diary back—he is going to write in it while I am gone on leave. Talked over things. He won't think I am unreasonable. I am.

Jan. 16, 1919—Thursday—went to breakfast, wrote a few letters. Got our leaves this a.m. Capt. Fuach and Lt. Bartlett brought them up. Took a bath and packed a few things. Elliott came out 1:30 p.m. We went out on South road—In room for a short time. Girls went to dance at Bornetble, 82nd Div. enlisted men. My sweetheart came just as girls were leaving for the dance. We stayed in dormitory—he left about eleven, said good-bye to him—leave for Paris tomorrow 3:45. Do not want to see him again before I leave—afraid I guess that I might cry. I should about die if I did. Our first separation, never thought I could care so much. My lover—went to window, just saw him going out the gate.

Jan 17, 1919—Friday—Up for breakfast—Conner helped me pack my carry-all—then dressed and Conner and I went down town—went over to see Colonel Dewal—Almost simultaneously saw Lt. Bartlet, Lt. Colsam, Capt. Marshall, Lt. Buddington, Major Rouch, Lt. Krog. Lt. Bartlett fixed things up so Conner could go with us. He is adjutant. Capt. Fox appeared and he told us a number of things concerning Paris and Nice. Lt. Bartlett and Capt. Fox brought us home in the Colonel's car. Stopped and got my shoes and Ulster. Boots wants to go—Bartlett said he'd see—Conner and Cantu are not going. Boots got permission. At 1:30 left hospital. 2:45 stopped and got my dress and Boutillier went. On our way to station saw Elliott and a nurse, it is the one he told me about, Florence Springer. He had a telegram from her saying she would stop to see him on her way somewhere. I don't like it but I love my skinny and know he is all right. Capt. Fox, Lieut. Bartlett and Favinger were at the station. Lieut. Bartlett took my suitcase and was most attentive. Did not have fair to pay and we are supposed to have hotel bills etc. paid but I doubt it.

Met some very nice American sailors who are stationed near Brent also a mailman. He showed us pictures of the ocean, depth mines, and submarine chasers. Mail carrier gave us magazines etc. we had a good dinner. Time went very fast we reached Paris about 8:20. We left the station about nine. French baggage man was so funny. Took a taxi wanted a trolley we laughed and laughed. Had a one hour delay trying to get a taxi and right hotel, Hotel Normandy. Washburn had telegraph for reservations for us. There are 10 Hotel Normandy's in Paris. Fortunately we got the right one first. Finke and I are together in room 88, Cobafpells with Greenman, Boots with Connor, and Bartling with Edgar. Finke and I fussed around in front of mirrors, so long since we had one to use. Got Elliott's picture out hadn't known whether I want it or not. Wonder why I do trust him and feel this way given I'm jealous a little because he told me about this girl.

January 18, 1919—Saturday—Miss my precious silly got up at 8 a.m. dressed hurriedly and went to breakfast Chapels, Greenmen, Finke and I left without much. Went with Connor and Boots to R.C. Commentary for shoes. Each got a pair and went back to the hotel for dinner, had our tickets, some cards, and ice cream. Rested had dinner and went to grand opera "Cuida" The Opera house is beautiful. I love him. Previous thoughts I will not write.

January 19, 1918—Sunday—Up at 8 a.m. Connor came in before I was dressed, she waited, we went down to the dining room. Boots was patiently waiting there, then we and the other girls went to the station and got our reservations for Nice. Bartling lost Edgar's and her travel orders. After station we went to Hotel de Pavilion (Y.M.C.A headquarters) expecting to take a sightseeing trip but as there was nothing but Versailles trip we decided to leave it until our return. Got a taxi and went with an American boy, first to see the most wonderful paintings, "Parthenon of War" at Rue University. From there to the Eiffel Tower and across to the Trocaders, a magnificent auditorium and exposition building. The Seine not wide nor long but very beautiful. Visited Napoleon's tomb it was not entirely uncovered (sandbags) Chapel and back to hotel. Had a very good dinner. Packed my suitcase and put Connor's and Boot's shoes, and Edgar's sugar. Boots came in, I dressed in a hurry and we left in a taxi for Notre Dame. I was provoked at Greenman, she went with us back to the hotel. Boots and I went out got cocoa and ice cream went back to the hotel for a rest in bed until 5 p.m. Boots came in said all were going to eat across the street, hurried-had steak, french—fried potatoes, tea and oranges. Connor, Boots and I got in taxi together, Bartling and Edgar in another we laughed at Connor trying to stop the driver to ask if he knew where he was going. Police stopped him to make him light up. We had a serious time finding a seat. Connor and I sat with three other nurses and a Lieut. Doherty. Connor, Finke, Greenman and Chappels played "500", Boots and Bartling had headache. I read. Just a month ago I met my lover boy hardly seems possible it is such a short time ago.

January 20, 1919—Monday—Had the usual night on a French train somewhat warmer. officers were well behaved. Sandwiches from the Red Cross had them about 10. We all went to breakfast, stood in line for ages then were served bread old and stale cold meat and cocoa. Talked to some men who knew Ms. Morgan and some other Camp Lewis girls also knew Lieut. Brindjove. think these girls were at Dijohn. The scenery is beautiful, walked around the station at Marse saw some well-dressed women wonder if they were Americans. Got into Nice about 4:10. Went to Westminster Hotel—very fine—on English Promenade. Finke and I are together pay 19 francs a day-the other four are together and in a front room. Boots and Connor near us. We have a lovely room, great long mirrors and the most luxurious bed. Not having any lunch—just put on train, we were extremely hungry—ate everything put before me, spinach was so good managed to get some vinegar with our French-English. Set in parlor a while talked to another nurse.

Almost 9, Finke and Chappels went to enlisted men's dance. Boots, Connor and I to officers dance. Lieut. Alan very nice.

Three other officers visited we had some cocoa and sandwiches while with them. Met three more they all insisted on walking home with us. Flannery made dates for tomorrow lunch at two and dance 4 p.m. after tea had a good time. Came in and took our orders down to be stamped Finkes washed hair and clothes—bad flue in fireplace. Went in Connor's and Boot's room they were still in bed at 10 a.m. had their breakfast brought up. Had lunch at about 12:30 then Boots, Connor and I went over to the British YMCA. A beautiful casino of pre-war days set out over water (Mediterranean) the enlisted men headquarters and place of entertainment. Boots met a boy she knew. We completely forgot our dates. Went down town to get some patent leather belts but came home with wine, eggs and cheese. Boots wanted to meet her friend at four so we hurried back. Connor and I later went to casino to get some candy. Met Miss Dorrity—talked a while with her, saw Edgar she told us we had to go down and get our transportations, we returned to hotel hired a cabby, he charged seven francs (rascal) and went to R.T.O.

Captain Ford was nice but slightly fresh—he walked home with us, showing us a short interesting way. After dinner Boots, Connor and I went to Casino to dance. All came home with someone, I with a very nice fellow. Didn't see Miss. Dorrity. Rounsaville is with Base 72—A beautiful night—the lighted Casino, the blue, blue ocean and the loveliest of moons—wish my Skinny could be here. I have his picture on the mantel Fiske says she likes it there most as much as I do—says she could almost kiss it good night. She is so quite, sounded funny. Got our tickets today for Friday.

January 22,1919—Wednesday—Finke and I got up early for breakfast—fussed about and got ready for trip to Grasse—Left Cooks, with "Steamboat Bill" as our driver about ten o'clock. Fiske admired the cemetery but didn't like the little houses. Just as we passed a bridge. On the way up the differential was stripped by something or other on our car and we had to change rides. Boots and I decided to stay together; Finke sailed down. They had walked up road a ways viewing a water fall—Crucifix on top most point—said she was going to stay. It turned out that Conner and I got in with a party of four officers and one nurse. Had a dandy trip. We got back around 4:30. Caption Dawson and Miss Hedge asked us to have some wine with them in the lobby of the hotel, we did and went with them to officers Y. to dance—Met Wickett, Reynolds, Jefferson and Lavler. Dance a lot. Lt. Wilder very nice to me, asked if he could take me to the dance tonight, "perhaps." Caption Wickett came up to hotel and had dinner with us. Lt Davis came over to our table and asked me to go to Conner and to get Finke for his friend, Lt. Atkinson. I hardly knew what to do—Finke was going to enlisted men Y.M.C.A so I asked Boots to go with Atkinson and Bartling with Wilden (he had come in the meantime) and I with Davis-he followed me everywhere. I shall ditch him-even chased me up the stairs when I went to see Connor. Seemed to think I would slip off, I felt like it. He really is nice and we had a wonderful evening.

Casino is a gorgeous affair. Went to movies there and between acts sat out at little tables in a mammoth room, where short acts, singing etc. were going on—severed drinks—"I drank lemonade

and Davis was nice—did too. To late for dancing at O.Y.—back to
hotel in lobby awhile—then to bed. Davis wanted me to make date
told him I had a previous ones. I can evade him-he is too attentive
and persistent to meet me and I don't want any one man hanging
around.

Jan. 23, 1919—Thursday—Finke got up early, others all
went on Monte Carlo trip—I got up at 8:00. Boots came over all
dressed—we had breakfast in their room then went down town. Got
our tickets at R.T.O. Got some stockings at a very sweet looking
store—went thru Notre Dame Church. A funeral mass had just been
said. Went across to large department store. Boots and Conner got
sweaters and I a bath robe. An Englishman took us up to the Roof
Garden-a wonderful view. Took a cab home. After dinner spent a
short time in Chapple's and Greeman's room. Then Connor and I
went to look for flower market and Russian cathedral-did not find
them. Met Miss Martin (Camp Lewis girl) and Miss. Coan. Went
to British U.N.C.A. had ice cream and coco with two boys then to
the casino and danced. Boys walked to hotel with us—came back
at eight—went to Mones and danced after—good time. Received
a telegram from my sweetheart—found out from Miss.Washburn
where I was-was awfully glad—put it away very close to me-looked
at it again and again. Still don't feel that I want to write to him I love
him so much, but he is not going to know how much.

Camp Lewis
Nora Daly 1918

Jan. 24, 1919—Friday—"O how I hate to get up in the morning" Conner called me at 7:15—Boots, she and I had breakfast together—and then started on our second mountain trip. We had seat in bus all to ourselves—a wonderful trip. Monte Carlo is quite magnificent. Saw lavish baths and electric massage room. Do not know proper name. I got on a horse (a wooden one) and got "shook" plenty—two fellows were with us—orchestra, dance.

The few villages in mountains are so seemingly isolated and every spot is cultivated. We had lunch upon reaching Monte Carlo at Café on Cornicle Blvd. Had drinks at café de Paris later. Went in lobby of Hotel de Paris. The Park—landscaping all about Casino is beautiful.

Back to Nice 4:30p.m. Conner and I went looking for cameos and flower market, neither again. Conner got a mural. Met Edgar and Bartling they said we have to register out and get out travel order. Checked out, walked down, cab coming back. Washed my hair in Conner's room—intended to stay in but Boots and I went down to Y.—got some sandwiches, cocoa, and cookies for lunch—stayed and danced until nearly 10 o'clock—then boys walked to hotel with us. Fiske and I packed after getting in—we laughed until we were sick trying to get my old suit case in shape.

Jan. 25, 1919—Saturday—We were called at 5 o'clock (time to catch train) I was so sleepy—asked Fiske to get up, she was on outside or I'd surely fall over her—she didn't sleep it was such an effort, we both went sound asleep—woke with a start at 5:30—scrambling and giggling it was funny. Man came to get our suit cases, we were still in our gowns—he disappeared "tout sweet" Fiske is so particular and finicky. I waited for her and then she lost her powder puff. I walked to elevators and when we reached lobby it was ten of six and the other girls—bus were gone—I had the travel orders or lengthily ticket for all, clerk said we wouldn't get cab unless we found one on street. We dashed madly out and fortunately a cab was just passing empty-hailed it and told him to take us to the station. Tried to infer on him our hurry, with our limited French, beau camp toot sweet. I shall never forget that funny noisy ride. Gave the cabby 100 francs and grabbed our suitcases and ran into station. He was still ejaculating and waving his arms, never will know what for, more money or the fact that it was to much. The girls were so relived when they saw us. They hardly knew what they were going to do but were trusting providences. I had to drag my suitcase by the strap, the handle was broken think it alone saved us from the girls ire.

Took carriage to Leigue. Connor, Boots and I together Some Captain and a Lieutenant. Captain looked a grouch, but he turned out to be great. Had a Frenchman in carriage, after he left a doctor friend of the Captain came a Lt. Thomas nicest man. I had candy and we ate lunch of sardines and canned meat. The boys got some bread and had a picnic eating it. Lt. Thomas took our picture at

St. Andre. Brought me a postcard with handkerchief. French were selling at station. Got into League and it was so cold-I was coughing-felt miserable-went out to look for lunch. Met Lt. Davis, Lt. Thomas, and Capt Ziegler came out of no where and asked us to have lunch with them. Then dinner and movies. My cough was so bad. Lt. Thomas insisted I go. Glad I did. They had a special table made up at Hotel de Paris and a excellent dinner. the lights in our Hotel went out just as we entered. Lt. Thomas took us to our room, tried to find it with a candle. Got boy to light our fireplace he was kind, I was most sick fireplace helped oceans. We undressed and set there., tried to get warm. Took my lovers picture in front of the fireplace with me. It is a comfort-we then got in bed together—put me in middle—was nearly crushed and I got up about 2 a.m. and got in the other bed. Never was such a cold bed.

Jan. 26, 1919—Sunday—Conner woke up a couple of times, fearing we would over sleep—got up at what we thought was 7:15 but it was however earlier—6:15. We dressed, packed, ugh it was cold—down to breakfast to Paris Montparnasse—omelet & chocolate—paid our bill—hotel—met Capt Zigler he was looking for R.T.O. At delicatessen shop we got more dates, had our pie and cheese with us—made for bus—had to wait for Tommy, Davey, Park, Jeff and Fatty. Arrived just in time but the carriages were about filled we had to stand in the aisle. Changed at St. Auban we three got seats and room for all the baggage and Lt. Robinson's roll. The boys looked us up as soon as we reached Veynes where we had an excellent dinner. From Veynes we were all together until we reached Grenoble. Lt. Thomas asked about my ring—the girls are teasing me about him—doesn't bother me. Got in enlisted men carriages—boys brought us sandwiches and oranges—we had dates & the enlisted boys had milk chocolate—so altogether we had a good lunch. One of these boys had been especially nice to me in Nice. Looked after me at Lyon—Good-bye to other boys. Had our orders stamped and walked to Hotel Bristol—just a short distance—trying to engage at taxi here is sometimes too great an effort. Washed and went to bed. After I put my sweetie out on table.

Jan. 27, 1919—Monday—Conner, Boots and I up about 10:00 a.m. Bath—Bartling and Edgar came in—up quite early. Fiske stayed in bed all day. Chapples came up to look for us as we were leaving for down town so she and Green went with us. Went up on train and directly to restaurant and had the most delicious dinner. Everything tasted so good and then we three went looking for bags. Conner, Boots got one—brought some stockings and bloomers. It was very cold and my feet were wet, had a hot foot bath and went to bed. Boots and Conner packed, then Boots got in with me and Conner in the other bed—stayed 5:30 were supposed to be out of room by 6:00. Dressed and with my baggage went down to lobby expecting to stay until train time but an M.P. told Bartling & Edgar to start for station between 7 and 8 ("Damned M.P.") So we all left got a good hot omelet and potatoes and chocolate—then to station thinking we could find a carriage, as M.P. interfered—but stood and walked and waited and were generally disgusted—were so cold & tired. It was dreadfully crowded as usual—they were nine where Conner, Edgar, Bartling and Boutilline. There were three Frenchmen and one French nurse. I got in with a red cross worker and four American officers. They were fine, I was comfortable and felt fortunate indeed.

Jan.28, 1919—Tuesday—Got into Paris about 10 a.m. Train late—cold and nasty—no taxi available then so went into station got ham sandwiches & chocolate. Went out on platform tipped a Frenchie 3 Francs to get a taxi—then the crazy old driver took us all over creation—wanted a 3 Fr. tip and 7 francs for fare. Couldn't get room at Petrogad so went to Mondial 5 Cite Bergere. Fiske, Boots, Conner and I together 14 Francs each. Got to hotel at 1 o'clock. Cleaned up a bit and set out for Red Cross supply station—got our waists, went to "Lafayette Galleries" big department store—belt and ties—tea room later—nothing to eat—found a dismal dinner—dinner not satisfactory. Bartling and Edgar had dinner with us—met them at the market before going to hotel. Boots, Conner and I went into another place—had chocolate, ham sandwiches and cakes. After reached hotel Conner and I walked to hotel de Pavilion 36-38 Rue de L'Echiquier to ask about trips to Versailles—going out there in a.m. Sent a telegram to Elliott. Cleaned up & packed.

Jan. 29, 191—Wednesday—Up about 7:30—had breakfast, got in taxi—went to Imolides Station, 35 cnturies—to V. When we got there found we couldn't go thru palace until 1:00 p.m. We walked all around garden—they are beautiful—very formal. I was cold and afraid of taking more cold. Boots and I decided to return—came back on electric—met a nice policeman, had an excellent dinner. We paid our hotel bill—I went to hair dresser with Boots while she had a marcel put in—got back and were just ready to leave when the other four returned—went to station and are on our way to Le Maus and my sweetheart. I shall be heartsick if he is not there—Conner and I are together—two American officers and one Frenchmen—one officer got off at noon—other officer is with a German prisoner. Chappels, Fiske, & Boots are in a carriage, same coach with some enlisted men & one Frenchie. Edgar, Bartling and Greeman are in another coach—8 a.m. Hope there is a letter from home and one from John and Joseph. Reached Le Maus expecting to find Elliott, not a soul there—we finally found someone to take us out to Annex—no place else to go—our group were gone but doubly up in big ward already full of nurses, we had a rest of sorts.

Jan. 30, 1919—Thursday—Fiske and I shared a cot—good thing we are both fairly small. Got up with the surety that I would see my lover boy soon, very soon but he didn't come all day. I was getting peeved. Didn't realize that French telegrams are slow—and that we were in Le Maus before he got my wire. Bartling, Boots, Conner and I went down town in a.m.—shopped—tried to find out about shoes and caps at Y.M.C.A. etc. Ran into Burns, Miss Washburn, & Capt. Roundell. Burns left me nearly broken hearted by telling me before she ever said hello that my brothers came the day after I left. I never was so miserable in my life. Miss. Washburn said an ambulance would be right in and we were sent out to the Annex—had our dinner and as no one had come Bartling and I went down town—weren't there but a short time when Chaplets came chasing us to bring us back to Annex as we were to leave by 3 p.m. We finished our shopping however and then we waited until 6:30 or more and then Elliott came with an ambulance for us, and I wasn't very nice to him, and I scolded good and I was all together miserable that I had missed John and Joseph. Nothing Elliott could say would help but I was weary and provoked. Seemed good to find a comfortable place at camp hospital 101 for us. Girls went to dance at 52 but Elliott and I stayed home. I slept with Borsch

January 31, 1919—Thursday—Fixed a bed in dormitory. Went with Elliott this P.M. and evening-long walk.

Feb1, 1919 Friday—Wire from that girl!

Feb.2, 1919—Saturday—Letter from that crazy woman telling me things about Elliott, saying she had loved him for years he is hers. That I must give him up. Didn't realize that there were women like that in this world. Such has been fiction.

February 3, 1919—Sunday—When Elliott and I were returning from our walk, just as we were turning in that crazy girl saw us and was getting out of an ambulace, she had coxed someone to bring her out here from Le Maus. She called to Elliott when she saw us keeping on and Elliott made me go with him. Oh I didn't want to. Said she wanted to talk to Elliott and he told her to go back and leave him alone, she put on a faint and he grabbed her roughly, I thought by the collar and put her in the ambulance seat and told the driver take her to Colonel Daval and he would be right over. Elliott took me to ward, got Miss Washburn and she and Colonel Daval started to Le Maus with her but she took on so and said she would kill herself, they brought her back afraid to trust her alone. Miss Washburn put her in a room and put nurse on duty. She raved and raved. I was in the room across. Mims and Brosch stayed with me, although Elliott insisted Miss Wasburn take me to Le Maus. He was afraid she might do something to me. They talked to her and tried to quiet her, she raved about me being a Catholic etc.

February 4, 1919—Monday—They took her to La Maus today, found some friend and she was sent to a Base Hospital. Elliott wrote to head nurse.

February 5, 1919—Friday—The boys whistled and sung this and we loved it, Edgar will not sing it when the boys are around unless they start it. She is afraid they might think, perhaps she might be vain.

The Rose of No Mans Land

There is a rose that grows in no mans land

And it is wonderful to see

Though its sprayed with tears

It will live for years

In my garden of memories

It's the one red rose, the soldier knows

It's the work of the Masters hand

Mid the wars great curse

Stands the Red Cross nurse

She is the Rose of no mans land

March 1, 1919—Saturday—My diary was neglected. I can remember all our lovely walks, the beautiful days spent together-rain or shine, they were all wonderful. Can see the road, the trees and small groves, our star, the many paths and by-ways of the country, around the little hill we use to climb and look over the surrounding country. The French house we had omelets and french fried potatoes, the firsts time in their living room, there after in their parlor. The beautiful bed of yellow wild flowers, I wondered what they were. The frog crocking in the evening. The beautiful house.

March 2, 1919—Sunday—Elliott wrote this in my diary. Nora didn't go to church. I played poker and lost. Dinner was certainly punk. Rained, we have to be home in 25 minutes. Rochester 6000 miles

March 3, 1919—Elliott and I left for town about 9a.m. Accomplished so much. Elliott brought a green slip and sweater. Large white collar, it is darling. Arrived at nurses quarters about noon. Miss Gjillum told me my brother had been at hospital while we were gone. I was nearly frantic fearing I had missed him entirely. Elliott got the Colonel's car and we went right back to Le Maus. After trying to eat. I think Captain Randell, Major Wyrahen and Buddington went in also. Went up to 52 and I remember got out at big square in La Maus and when we reached the sidewalk, there was John. We were with him until four o clock. He left at 4:40 for St. Nalo.

March 14, 1919—Friday—Brosch left on leave.

March 16, 1919—Sunday—7:00 mass. Elliott played ball, Jerry's birthday, wrote to C. Lynch.

March 17, 1919—Monday—St. Patrick's Day found a bit of green.

March 19, 1919—Wednesday—Rained, Elliott and I went through my Red Cross bag then went to supper early. I heard Boutellier say "Daly" then something about her knowing soon enough. I immediately thought of dreadful things and of Elliott in particular, went into quarters, wanted to lie down and cry. Elliott came in a few minutes to tell me he had received word that he was to leave Evac. # 11. I was sick, no one can know of the ache in my heart. I can't be without him, my sweetheart, The days will be so empty and long. Went to haunted house and later in office of mumps' ward.

March 20, 1919—Thursday—Half day. we went up on hill-found a dry place by a big tree. Elliott marked the tree with our

113

initials. How can I spend the time without him. I should be brave, he needs me to be and I can't. I want to hold him back, keep him here with me. My lover, you can't know how I love you.

March 21, 1919—Friday—Morning hours—Went for a walk, and found some peach blossoms and violets-We were hoping orders would not come. Set in nurses living room until two. I went on duty. And shortly after Elliott got his orders to report to headquarters. I felt as if he couldn't go—something must stop it. He went over to office, came back in a few minutes, packed, back at 4:30 stayed until supper time.

March 22, 1919—Saturday—Yule took my lover in early came on ward at 8:30. 10:25 I got a note given by Solly by Yule, Elliott telling me where he was, at Celort for the present—attending Surgeons office, Le Maus. My own lover—happy you are near—even tough it may be only a while. He came out at noon to get his baggage—back at 6:30—my first evening without him.

March 23, 1919—Sunday—Elliott out late until p.m. stayed with me until 10:00.

March 24, 1919—Monday—Out again—back at 9.
He is O.D (officer of the day) tomorrow and so he brought me a letter to read and to have for tomorrow night. And so every night my precious would ride out in a big truck to see me and go back between 9 and 10. We had afternoons together frequently. Elliott took on the morning work at surgeons office and thereby is free p.m. to be with me. Excepting when O.D. then I always had a letter and one ready for him. I love him.

April 4, 1919—Elliott took my diary to write in it. With all the uncertainty about our moves he is afraid we will be separated again. Rather the fear he might be where we couldn't see each other. He insist we get married. Went to headquarters—almost made me talk to Miss Washburn—I don't want to marry over here. Silly reason,

I know. I shouldn't lose a day I can spend with him life is so short and I want him always. I'm sure but I want him to be sure—he thinks I'm silly when I say that and he becomes a little provoked. However it seems best way to me now—to wait until we get home. Until I meet his people and he my people. I think they will like it better that way—we will be surer of our happiness. I shall see if it is possible for me to go home—Brosch will go with me.

April, 1919—We have asked to be sent home there is nothing here now to be done but wait. Mrs. Washburn, our chief is going with us, and Burns, Brosch of course, I mean by us Baittling and Edgar—we are six.

May 13, 1919—Heard our orders were coming.

May 14, 1919—Received our orders this noon for home. Leave Friday for the states. I got shoes, rubbers, and raincoat. Elliott and I walked out to the old French home said goodbye to them. I think my heart is breaking—I can't bear to leave him and I want to for I know it is best. I was afraid I would marry over here and we even picked out the place where we would like to spend our honeymoon—almost wore a map out. I do know that I shall never leave him again. I love him so.

May 15, 1919—Thursday—Our last day together in France It can't be for the best to leave him ever—nothing worth while without him. We went out and it rained. Enlisted boys had dinner and I couldn't go. Elliott stayed until 11 p.m. Someone drove a motorcycle out for him. Elliott wrote home sometime ago to his dad and their state senator to use their influence to get him home—so perhaps I shall have him again soon.

May 16, 1919—As we were leaving our quarters a regimental band played "Till We Meet Again" It came rather faintly through the trees and breeze and if it were possible I think I would have stayed. I was so lonely at leaving my precious behind. He was at the station and stayed until we left—about 12:15. Words can't describe how awfully bad it was to leave him. Sent him a letter at Femues, two cards at Morlaix. Reached Brest at 10:15 p.m. Registered at station and headquarters—was then taken to camp hospital #118—nurses infirmary—had a good rest.

May 17, 1919—breakfast—up town and I sent a telegram to Elliott, John, and Joseph. Walked around some——wrote to Elliott, mailed it in hospital at noon. Napped and after waiting for some time we came out to Kerhnon about 4:30—everything fine—Brosch and I have rooms together. Nurses having a big living room in one barracks building—showers, bath, plenty of reading etc. Wrote to Elliott.

March 18, 1919—Sunday—Went to mass—got a pass—went for a walk. It really is lovely here—the ocean—the quaint very neat and fine looking peasants. Wish I were here to enjoy it. Wrote to John, Joseph, and Elliott. Cards to Conner and O' Conner.

May 19, 1919—Monday—Wrote home, washed hair after supper—then went to Camp Pontanazer saw Mary Cunningham—Guard was kind enough to let me into hospital. Good time at dance. Wrote to Elliott's mother today and of course one to my sweetheart.

May 20, 1919—Tuesday—Sent Elliott a letter—saw a group of girls leave about 8:30 a.m. shortly after we got orders to leave in 15 minutes. Brosch and I gave R. C. girls telegrams to send. My emotions were varied Tried to be awfully glad to be going home, I was, but my precious sweetheart, I did not want to leave him. Got on board not a very fine boat "Grap Waldersee" A German boat—2nd class—and its 2nd trip. Edgar and I with two others are in one cabin—Broach in next with others. Had lunch and dinner.

May 21, 1919—Wednesday—Waited on breakfast for so long-then when I took a taste of grapefruit I left the table. Stayed in bed nearly all day. Major Conley came in to see what I wanted to eat-grape fruit toast and grape juice.

May 22, 1919—Thursday—Up at 6;00,Edgar too—went to breakfast with her—feel very much better. Major Conley talked with me awhile. Sea very rough—to cabin-sick and vomited. Never felt quite so miserable or lonely in my life.

May 23, 1919—Friday—Hard time getting up—no breakfast. Dressed ate a pickle-piece of bread. Went up on deck, cold but managed to stay until lunch—ate a little back on deck. Set down with the rest of the family.

May 24, 1919—Saturday—Read some things and danced in the evening.

May 25,1919—Sunday—Mass at 9:30 in dining room Borsch-Burns and I went. Darn men positively won't leave you alone. Came down to cabin about twelve. Back to rest and maybe write.

May 26, 1919—Monday—Took a bath and played cards, hearts—Danced.

May 27, 1919—Tuesday—Sat around, read—Lt. Donahue is so nice to me. He really is a fine fellow.

May 28, 1919—Wednesday—Finished "Garden of Allah". In cabin all p.m. went to enlisted men's dance. Burns was nasty—took my rain hat and threw it overboard. The men want to be with Betty and I and they are jealous. I think I am about through with this bunch of old cats.

May 29, 1919—Thursday—Manicured nails, sewed on collar and cuffs. wrote to Johnny Johnson—took a bath—Danced on deck with Lt. Donahue and Paul. Set on deck with Lt. Donahue awhile after—Lt. Paul stayed with us awhile. Burns and Edgar passed several times and I suppose I will catch it. Lt. Donahue is very fine, otherwise I wouldn't and he knows I'm very much taken up with someone—understands. We have enjoyed each other.

May 30, 1919—Friday—Storm-no one allowed on deck got pretty well sprinkled before I left.

May 31, 1919—Saturday—quieter, beautiful sunset and new moon. Movies and walk with Lt. Donahue. He has some beautiful prints, why didn't I get some.

June 1, 1919—Sunday—Most wonderful morning-saw black fish-looked black-supposed porpoise—band—Lt. Donahue. My sweetheart I am always thinking of you.

June 2, 1919—Monday—Docked-America-Home States-Hoboken, N.J. 9.30 A.M. Went across in yacht to New York. Red Cross ambulance took us to Polyclinic for examination for cooties imagine I would think a nurse could keep her self clean most any place she happened to be. Don't imagine they ever found any. I had a few just once in France but just one day. Red Cross ambulance took us to Hotel Albert—registered filled out questionnaire. After lunch rested awhile. Cablegram to Elliott-he is to let boys know. Miss. Washburn, Brosch and I went out for a little while. Got a big A and our overseas pin. Then took two baths—it is warm—to bed early.

Distance from Brent to New York-3140 miles

Wed. 21	first day	170 miles
Thurs. 22	2nd day	250 miles
Fri. 23	3rd day	241 miles
Sat. 24	4th day	275 miles
Sun. 25	5th day	290 miles
Mon. 26	6th day	284 miles

Tues. 27	7th day	291 miles
Wed. 28	8th day	241 miles
Thurs. 29	9th day	257 miles
Fri. 30	10th day	201 miles
Sat. 31	11th day	218 miles
Sun. June 1	12th day	271 miles
Mon. June 2	Docked	

June 3, 1919—Write to Elliott everyday. Had a general physical examination. Shopping got a hat, dress, and suitcase—things I needed.

June 4, 1919—Wednesday: Hair shampooed and marceled. Were paid. Got my suitcase and packed some. Brosch did her hair, permanent too, and we were almost late for our checks.

June 5, 1919—Thursday—Signed for transportation to get my ticket for Elmira, Miss. Washburn and I took bus ride. I left hotel for Lackawana Station about 10:30. I had to cross ferry.

June 6, 1919—Friday—Train left 2 a.m., got into Elmira at 9:25 a.m. Aunt Mollie and Anna were at station. Uncle Tom's day out. He got in about 9:30 p.m.

June 7, 1919—Saturday—Talked and visited so much. Rest in p.m. Dinner at Mrs. Esney—bridge—good time

June 8,1919—Sunday—6:30 a.m.—went to 7:30 mass. Mrs. Hogan and Stella came in and a friend of Uncle Toms, Charlie Conklin—chicken dinner and short rest. A wonderful car ride all over Elmira. Lunch at 7:00. Up to Mrs. Fritz Patrick—Joseph and Helen—11:30 home and bed. On our way up to F we stooped into Healy's—met Joe, Mary and Mrs. Healy.

June 9, 1919—Monday—Telegram home and to Ryans at Oxford. Anna and I went shopping. Stopped into Price's on our way back. Met Gerald and Mrs. Price, his mother. Alice, his sister, came over later. Went to hear Paulist Choristers in evening. Met Mr. and Mrs. Maloney. At street car met Clair Brafley and Stella Ryan. George Ryan called while I was gone.

June 10, 1919—Tuesday—Uncle Tom out-down town brought pumps and stockings. Prices up to Murphy's.

June 11,1919—Wednesday—Aunt Mollie and I to Oxford-George met us, went to Kitties all the luaus is in the evening.

June 12, 1919—Thursday—George took us to Sherburne-lunch-out to Aunt Ellen when we returned—all night there.

June 14, 1919—Saturday—Merrites for dinner. R.D. for supper
June 15, 1919—Sunday—Herberts—long ride-Aunt Mollie back to Elmira., back to Kitties—Aunt Ellen picnic dinner-Merritts. Nian, Lenna, Dorothy, Frank H. and I

June 16, 1919—Monday—Sidney, Merritt's wife, lived here before marriage—taught. Sent a telegram to Roche—went thru cheese factory. Left for Albany-reached there at 6:30. Roche met me, to his home—dinner—stayed with his sister, Mrs. Ryan that night.

June 17, 1919—Tuesday—Trip to Lenox, Mass. Visited his brother, a priest, at Revenue or Ravenna, a little town near Albany. He, a sister of Rocke, and a friend took trip with us.

June 18, 1919—Wednesday—Back to New York on steamer. The trip from Albany beautiful. Man was nice to me. Knowing we would never meet again—he asked about my ring knowing it was French. Told me how much he had cared for someone-said under the adverse circumstances and the most trying could not be other than true love. I did not need to care what he said nor anyone else, still it made me feel good as I have a feeling people will say a war romance, and doubt its sincerity. Thursday, June 19: Start home 5:50 p.m.

June 20, 1919—Wednesday—Due in Chicago at 9:10—Leave 2:00 a.m.

June 21,1919—Saturday, Home, Mama, Jerry, Rochester

Afterward

Verdum—Energy, courage, and faith which held this city together even when for months one of the strongest outside fortresses was in the German's hands. Verdum barring its ruins is a lovely little town with a fine old citadel to crown its heights and quays along the river that made one stop and to lounge along them and dream. There are old churches and old facades and quite charming streets and clean, comfortable hotel. One feels the drama of its siege though on every side buildings are rising from the ruins.

Europe Will Change

In the exhumation of the bodies of Edith Cavell and the Belgian nurse who were shot to death as spies, the finding in the same grave with them is the German soldier Miss Cavell had nursed and who refused to shoot her. "There is a choice'" rose in the Thiergarten in Berlin that is named for Edith Cavell.

Nora Elizabeth Daly (Posthumously)

WINDSOR CASTLE.

Soldiers of the United States, the people of the British Isles welcome you on your way to take your stand beside the Armies of many Nations now fighting in the Old World the great battle for human freedom.

The Allies will gain new heart & spirit in your company.

I wish that I could shake the hand of each one of you & bid you God speed on your mission.

George R.I.

April 1918.

Wilson, the greatest war
leader of them all.

This story has a happy ending

Nora Elizabeth Daly
Elliott Sheldon Stong

Were joined in love September 19,1919 in
Saint John Church in Rochester, Minn.

They raised three sons
John Elliott Stong
Paul Anthony Stong
David Daly Stong
Jack was the oldest, married Olive Foley had three children. In the
Air Force during World War II. Jack died about two years ago. He
owned a Music Store in Medford, Oregon

Paul was the middle son. Married Frances W. (Billie) Chisholm.
They had ten beautiful children-Eight girls and two boys. Paul
served in the Infantry during World War II. Carried mail for 30
years. Billie and I were married 65 years before we lost her on
May 8th, Mother's Day.

Dave was the youngest. He served in the Navy during World War
II. Married Loraine San Cartie, They had six beautiful children
David was a very special young doctor.

Jack and Dave are both dead now. My mother gave me the diary
and beautiful story above. To me it is so special that I am going to
try to get it printed.

GOD BLESS YOU ALL

Acknowledgements

First of all, Thank You Mom for such a beautiful writing. I would like to give a special "thank you" to Sarah Ramirez, my special grand daughter who spent many hours typing my Mom's writings and putting them on the computer, to send to the publisher. Also, Thanks to all my children and grandchildren who worked so hard to get it all ready.

God Bless you all.

List of Supplies etc.—needed   addresses

New York City

1 blanket   Madison Square3684
1 sweater
1 rain coat and hat
1 pair rubber boots   Columbia Luggage Shop
1 pair of shoes Travelers   Outfitters 279 ave
1 bathrobe
1 sleeping bag

Bet.29th 130 Street

Red Cross 222—4th Ave. 12th Floor

Larr Studio   20 E-14 Street

Identification photos

Trunk steamer
Suit Case
Pens-pins—hair pins and nets
Nail files

Handkerchief
Gloves
Insignia
Foot warmers

Stanley Supply Co.
1182-25 th Street

West 33rd.

Dark glasses bloomers
Bulk jersey petticoats
Dark brown silk stockings
Heavy socks
Towels
Money bag
Whisk broom
Underwear
Wrist watch

Major Dayluiff
Pier I 1310 River St
Red brick building River St
Is straight from funnel terminal

Finger prints

"Garnoff

money bags
34 D r 4TH Ave
Passport 554

St. Paul's Chapel
Trinity Church
2nt W 3RD Ave
Elevated
Train to Brooklin Bridge

Mrs. Honkanon, Ontario, Oregon had charged on way over and until or disembarkment into smaller groups.

Nius Binus—New Jersey
Brody
Chambers
Crombie
Stewart
Vandenberger
Daly—Rochester, Minn.
Kloggie
Mc Donald—Fargo, N.D.
A. Mc Donald—Denver, CO
McWilliams—Allentown, Pennsylvania
Knogle—Minneapolis, MN
Clearny—Chicago, IL
Young Kettles
Claudia—Garivn, Ohio
Post—Francis, Ohio
Gray—Graborn, Ohio
McCoy—Hernick, IL
Carter—Writz, Iowa
Zogarts—Shelby
Zishy—Welch
Bell—Rose, CA
Larkin—Detroit, MI
Hyslope—Ireland
Fitzgerald—Muldoon, Mass.
Goodwin—CA
Staton—Delborne, CN
Summers—CA
Croven—Lyden
Peterson—
Sannuelson—CA
Spurney—Ohio
Herbirn—Colo

Williams—Colo
Shaw—Canada
Lichsteris—Indianna
Firangsw—Iowa
Rynes—Troy, NY
Kach—Washington
Mueller—Washington
Kaulfman—
Vores—
Files—

Col. D.F. Disval
Maj. Bailey—Greensborough, PN
Maj. Rooch—Brooklyn, NY
Maj. Jordan—Alabama
Wyrisher—San Antonio, TX
Maj. Elliott—New York City, NY
Capt. Ranodell—New York City, NY
Capt. Wrchette—Los Angles, CA
Capt. Renolds—Katisville, MT
Capt. Finch—St. Louis, Missouri
Capt. Walker—New Jersey
Capt. Marshall—Columbus, OH
Capt. Styars—Richmond, VA
Capt. Hunter—Davenport, PA
Capt. Watts—Davenport, PA
Capt. Fox—Oklahoma City, OK
Capt. Shields—Troy, NY
Capt. S. Stong—Humbolt, Iowa
Capt. Calsh—New Jersey
Lt. Woodburry—
Lt. Henderson—New York, NY
Lt. Wheeler—Minnesota
Lt. Dunn—Columbus, OH
Lt. Brindom—Butte, MT
Lt. La Garide—Washington D.C.
Lt. Rondell—Boise, ID
Lt. Favinager—Abiom, IN
Lt. Bartlett—Chicago, IL
Lt. M. McDonald—Chicago, IL
Lt. Lawber—New York, NY
Lt. Buddington—Mass.

Made in the USA
Middletown, DE
16 September 2024

61017687R00090